Math

Practice Worksheets and Workbook for Adult Students

A learner-centered tool designed to help students practice and master the **four operations** while preparing them for CASAS Math GOALS 2, TABE 11 and 12, ACT, HiSET, GED tests, and IET programs.

Table of Contents

Answer All the Questions Below:

1.	2.	3.	4.	5.
5 + 9	4 + 4	2 + 7	3 + 5	1 + 3

6.	7.	8.	9.	10.
6 + 3	6 + 9	9 + 9	9 + 4	6 + 3

11.	12.	13.	14.	15.
5 + 0	5 + 3	2 + 6	7 + 3	2 + 3

16.	17.	18.	19.	20.
8 + 8	8 + 6	2 + 3	2 + 8	1 + 2

1.
$$9 \\ +\ 8$$

2.
$$7 \\ +\ 6$$

3.
$$7 \\ +\ 4$$

4.
$$1 \\ +\ 6$$

5.
$$3 \\ +\ 8$$

6.
$$3 \\ +\ 5$$

7.
$$1 \\ +\ 4$$

8.
$$4 \\ +\ 2$$

9.
$$6 \\ +\ 5$$

10.
$$6 \\ +\ 0$$

11.
$$6 \\ +\ 2$$

12.
$$0 \\ +\ 1$$

13.
$$5 \\ +\ 8$$

14.
$$1 \\ +\ 8$$

15.
$$7 \\ +\ 2$$

16.
$$4 \\ +\ 1$$

17.
$$0 \\ +\ 8$$

18.
$$3 \\ +\ 0$$

19.
$$6 \\ +\ 0$$

20.
$$2 \\ +\ 9$$

ADDITION

1-Digit

1.	2.	3.	4.	5.
4 + 2	6 + 3	3 + 4	3 + 9	6 + 1

6.	7.	8.	9.	10.
0 + 0	4 + 8	5 + 3	5 + 0	9 + 7

11.	12.	13.	14.	15.
0 + 2	9 + 7	7 + 2	0 + 1	5 + 9

16.	17.	18.	19.	20.
7 + 9	9 + 3	6 + 1	0 + 5	1 + 9

1.
$$\begin{array}{r} 0 \\ +\ 4 \\ \hline \end{array}$$

2.
$$\begin{array}{r} 5 \\ +\ 1 \\ \hline \end{array}$$

3.
$$\begin{array}{r} 3 \\ +\ 8 \\ \hline \end{array}$$

4.
$$\begin{array}{r} 3 \\ +\ 9 \\ \hline \end{array}$$

5.
$$\begin{array}{r} 6 \\ +\ 6 \\ \hline \end{array}$$

6.
$$\begin{array}{r} 9 \\ +\ 7 \\ \hline \end{array}$$

7.
$$\begin{array}{r} 5 \\ +\ 2 \\ \hline \end{array}$$

8.
$$\begin{array}{r} 8 \\ +\ 9 \\ \hline \end{array}$$

9.
$$\begin{array}{r} 0 \\ +\ 8 \\ \hline \end{array}$$

10.
$$\begin{array}{r} 7 \\ +\ 0 \\ \hline \end{array}$$

11.
$$\begin{array}{r} 9 \\ +\ 1 \\ \hline \end{array}$$

12.
$$\begin{array}{r} 6 \\ +\ 9 \\ \hline \end{array}$$

13.
$$\begin{array}{r} 7 \\ +\ 9 \\ \hline \end{array}$$

14.
$$\begin{array}{r} 1 \\ +\ 5 \\ \hline \end{array}$$

15.
$$\begin{array}{r} 9 \\ +\ 7 \\ \hline \end{array}$$

16.
$$\begin{array}{r} 0 \\ +\ 6 \\ \hline \end{array}$$

17.
$$\begin{array}{r} 4 \\ +\ 7 \\ \hline \end{array}$$

18.
$$\begin{array}{r} 5 \\ +\ 7 \\ \hline \end{array}$$

19.
$$\begin{array}{r} 5 \\ +\ 6 \\ \hline \end{array}$$

20.
$$\begin{array}{r} 6 \\ +\ 0 \\ \hline \end{array}$$

ADDITION

1.	2.	3.	4.	5.
46 + 77	95 + 23	28 + 59	46 + 85	87 + 58

6.	7.	8.	9.	10.
67 + 43	94 + 86	47 + 92	38 + 53	96 + 95

11.	12.	13.	14.	15.
24 + 72	87 + 14	23 + 85	63 + 34	55 + 43

16.	17.	18.	19.	20.
80 + 89	91 + 18	89 + 71	12 + 44	26 + 28

21.	22.	23.	24.	25.
19 + 76	63 + 73	65 + 65	65 + 69	57 + 28

26.	27.	28.	29.	30.
18 + 40	10 + 57	57 + 60	21 + 31	67 + 40

Answer All the Questions Below:

1.	2.	3.	4.	5.
92 + 53	73 + 52	77 + 11	77 + 51	90 + 10

6.	7.	8.	9.	10.
59 + 98	17 + 57	90 + 23	21 + 68	32 + 31

11.	12.	13.	14.	15.
62 + 81	27 + 35	52 + 60	39 + 88	18 + 68

16.	17.	18.	19.	20.
59 + 60	18 + 65	29 + 89	92 + 73	53 + 86

21.	22.	23.	24.	25.
39 + 35	69 + 43	86 + 86	89 + 27	46 + 12

26.	27.	28.	29.	30.
79 + 37	48 + 58	31 + 93	12 + 82	48 + 33

Answer All the Questions Below:

1. 27 + 78	**2.** 51 + 79	**3.** 87 + 44	**4.** 83 + 94	**5.** 11 + 88
6. 85 + 51	**7.** 67 + 80	**8.** 65 + 40	**9.** 13 + 80	**10.** 15 + 16
11. 58 + 42	**12.** 38 + 93	**13.** 23 + 83	**14.** 15 + 86	**15.** 64 + 38
16. 28 + 55	**17.** 82 + 55	**18.** 93 + 76	**19.** 73 + 52	**20.** 35 + 69
21. 80 + 24	**22.** 14 + 64	**23.** 85 + 29	**24.** 27 + 87	**25.** 79 + 49
26. 41 + 71	**27.** 45 + 75	**28.** 13 + 25	**29.** 85 + 27	**30.** 43 + 89

Answer All the Questions Below:

1. 84 + 77	**2.** 83 + 27	**3.** 32 + 25	**4.** 43 + 47	**5.** 50 + 40
6. 51 + 99	**7.** 28 + 36	**8.** 39 + 30	**9.** 52 + 67	**10.** 10 + 39
11. 98 + 29	**12.** 81 + 45	**13.** 46 + 81	**14.** 28 + 23	**15.** 94 + 73
16. 54 + 30	**17.** 71 + 73	**18.** 28 + 40	**19.** 90 + 53	**20.** 63 + 14
21. 44 + 27	**22.** 45 + 49	**23.** 67 + 86	**24.** 15 + 19	**25.** 51 + 98
26. 66 + 80	**27.** 55 + 26	**28.** 61 + 53	**29.** 12 + 72	**30.** 15 + 11

ADDITION

1. 47 + 61	2. 67 + 96	3. 28 + 84	4. 29 + 37	5. 63 + 75
6. 32 + 45	7. 96 + 91	8. 23 + 59	9. 60 + 83	10. 29 + 47
11. 11 + 36	12. 34 + 82	13. 47 + 86	14. 89 + 45	15. 92 + 94
16. 33 + 45	17. 13 + 45	18. 33 + 88	19. 61 + 19	20. 53 + 26
21. 83 + 31	22. 60 + 33	23. 41 + 82	24. 16 + 22	25. 47 + 13
26. 90 + 47	27. 16 + 74	28. 24 + 56	29. 68 + 70	30. 42 + 12

ADDITION

3-Digit

Answer All the Questions Below:

1. 515 + 726	**2.** 509 + 610	**3.** 567 + 608	**4.** 672 + 362	**5.** 711 + 743
6. 246 + 287	**7.** 476 + 665	**8.** 570 + 824	**9.** 584 + 985	**10.** 699 + 373
11. 885 + 134	**12.** 265 + 855	**13.** 865 + 633	**14.** 698 + 202	**15.** 126 + 353
16. 697 + 143	**17.** 455 + 792	**18.** 823 + 214	**19.** 498 + 969	**20.** 539 + 578
21. 540 + 146	**22.** 944 + 484	**23.** 494 + 749	**24.** 247 + 338	**25.** 128 + 783
26. 152 + 996	**27.** 727 + 896	**28.** 143 + 302	**29.** 229 + 793	**30.** 261 + 705

ADDITION

3-Digit

Answer All the Questions Below:

1. 693 + 333	**2.** 466 + 971	**3.** 447 + 375	**4.** 176 + 865	**5.** 904 + 599
6. 222 + 465	**7.** 690 + 706	**8.** 618 + 800	**9.** 656 + 791	**10.** 382 + 692
11. 411 + 621	**12.** 536 + 254	**13.** 581 + 690	**14.** 402 + 685	**15.** 617 + 525
16. 918 + 245	**17.** 712 + 211	**18.** 497 + 322	**19.** 630 + 582	**20.** 919 + 423
21. 387 + 424	**22.** 345 + 550	**23.** 229 + 729	**24.** 891 + 919	**25.** 896 + 648
26. 680 + 111	**27.** 163 + 412	**28.** 224 + 906	**29.** 615 + 446	**30.** 548 + 677

Answer All the Questions Below:

1. $707 + 683$	**2.** $532 + 733$	**3.** $543 + 755$	**4.** $299 + 455$	**5.** $135 + 944$
6. $409 + 423$	**7.** $443 + 737$	**8.** $688 + 655$	**9.** $771 + 369$	**10.** $774 + 658$
11. $776 + 934$	**12.** $324 + 128$	**13.** $284 + 799$	**14.** $988 + 640$	**15.** $284 + 310$
16. $279 + 278$	**17.** $890 + 428$	**18.** $499 + 742$	**19.** $975 + 180$	**20.** $209 + 379$
21. $701 + 556$	**22.** $267 + 798$	**23.** $141 + 582$	**24.** $555 + 789$	**25.** $417 + 248$
26. $622 + 847$	**27.** $294 + 761$	**28.** $969 + 732$	**29.** $862 + 293$	**30.** $337 + 179$

ADDITION

Answer All the Questions Below:

1.	2.	3.	4.	5.
915 + 929	542 + 299	534 + 312	757 + 180	539 + 556

6.	7.	8.	9.	10.
502 + 155	745 + 867	912 + 182	478 + 646	671 + 852

11.	12.	13.	14.	15.
550 + 668	512 + 473	203 + 838	574 + 195	912 + 605

16.	17.	18.	19.	20.
590 + 332	767 + 782	394 + 125	999 + 409	422 + 505

21.	22.	23.	24.	25.
919 + 509	617 + 201	965 + 871	803 + 176	725 + 568

26.	27.	28.	29.	30.
975 + 120	821 + 545	984 + 512	811 + 739	147 + 814

1.	2.	3.	4.	5.
674 + 278	114 + 969	838 + 479	662 + 144	128 + 619

6.	7.	8.	9.	10.
875 + 189	576 + 373	814 + 553	403 + 531	750 + 369

11.	12.	13.	14.	15.
352 + 826	668 + 802	776 + 549	755 + 850	545 + 554

16.	17.	18.	19.	20.
192 + 523	477 + 541	380 + 456	712 + 303	126 + 180

21.	22.	23.	24.	25.
188 + 464	532 + 923	394 + 202	417 + 694	300 + 702

26.	27.	28.	29.	30.
692 + 266	760 + 160	958 + 965	692 + 852	757 + 354

Answer All the Questions Below:

1.
```
    5,825
+   8,121
_________
```

2.
```
    5,077
+   8,582
_________
```

3.
```
    2,464
+   4,571
_________
```

4.
```
    3,775
+   8,477
_________
```

5.
```
    5,178
+   9,745
_________
```

6.
```
    4,402
+   3,768
_________
```

7.
```
    5,506
+   8,046
_________
```

8.
```
    5,758
+   2,867
_________
```

9.
```
    7,764
+   4,661
_________
```

10.
```
    9,565
+   7,698
_________
```

11.
```
    8,677
+   8,042
_________
```

12.
```
    2,247
+   5,583
_________
```

13.
```
    7,927
+   3,631
_________
```

14.
```
    8,041
+   4,459
_________
```

15.
```
    5,477
+   9,249
_________
```

16.
```
    4,241
+   8,131
_________
```

17.
```
    5,138
+   2,311
_________
```

18.
```
    4,804
+   1,989
_________
```

19.
```
    8,215
+   6,879
_________
```

20.
```
    8,165
+   6,512
_________
```

21.
```
    4,167
+   7,399
_________
```

22.
```
    4,426
+   6,478
_________
```

23.
```
    3,134
+   1,833
_________
```

24.
```
    2,662
+   5,461
_________
```

1.
$$\begin{array}{r} 2{,}165 \\ +\ 2{,}617 \\ \hline \end{array}$$

2.
$$\begin{array}{r} 7{,}662 \\ +\ 3{,}876 \\ \hline \end{array}$$

3.
$$\begin{array}{r} 8{,}201 \\ +\ 4{,}401 \\ \hline \end{array}$$

4.
$$\begin{array}{r} 8{,}373 \\ +\ 2{,}738 \\ \hline \end{array}$$

5.
$$\begin{array}{r} 6{,}430 \\ +\ 2{,}220 \\ \hline \end{array}$$

6.
$$\begin{array}{r} 2{,}776 \\ +\ 7{,}125 \\ \hline \end{array}$$

7.
$$\begin{array}{r} 6{,}751 \\ +\ 3{,}571 \\ \hline \end{array}$$

8.
$$\begin{array}{r} 6{,}103 \\ +\ 4{,}322 \\ \hline \end{array}$$

9.
$$\begin{array}{r} 9{,}715 \\ +\ 3{,}056 \\ \hline \end{array}$$

10.
$$\begin{array}{r} 2{,}577 \\ +\ 8{,}355 \\ \hline \end{array}$$

11.
$$\begin{array}{r} 5{,}031 \\ +\ 7{,}029 \\ \hline \end{array}$$

12.
$$\begin{array}{r} 9{,}090 \\ +\ 5{,}319 \\ \hline \end{array}$$

13.
$$\begin{array}{r} 5{,}876 \\ +\ 2{,}772 \\ \hline \end{array}$$

14.
$$\begin{array}{r} 4{,}530 \\ +\ 5{,}512 \\ \hline \end{array}$$

15.
$$\begin{array}{r} 5{,}706 \\ +\ 5{,}056 \\ \hline \end{array}$$

16.
$$\begin{array}{r} 2{,}855 \\ +\ 6{,}083 \\ \hline \end{array}$$

17.
$$\begin{array}{r} 4{,}733 \\ +\ 4{,}391 \\ \hline \end{array}$$

18.
$$\begin{array}{r} 3{,}816 \\ +\ 7{,}357 \\ \hline \end{array}$$

19.
$$\begin{array}{r} 6{,}635 \\ +\ 1{,}736 \\ \hline \end{array}$$

20.
$$\begin{array}{r} 3{,}823 \\ +\ 2{,}033 \\ \hline \end{array}$$

21.
$$\begin{array}{r} 1{,}904 \\ +\ 5{,}238 \\ \hline \end{array}$$

22.
$$\begin{array}{r} 6{,}111 \\ +\ 3{,}348 \\ \hline \end{array}$$

23.
$$\begin{array}{r} 6{,}811 \\ +\ 8{,}283 \\ \hline \end{array}$$

24.
$$\begin{array}{r} 5{,}824 \\ +\ 5{,}256 \\ \hline \end{array}$$

ADDITION

4-Digit

1.	2.	3.	4.
3,678 + 9,338	7,175 + 6,768	6,628 + 8,454	5,776 + 5,791

5.	6.	7.	8.
9,049 + 1,944	6,531 + 5,080	3,610 + 4,410	8,288 + 2,026

9.	10.	11.	12.
2,254 + 8,864	8,131 + 8,732	9,369 + 6,461	8,051 + 1,601

13.	14.	15.	16.
4,619 + 3,258	7,189 + 1,832	2,524 + 8,931	8,830 + 9,788

17.	18.	19.	20.
1,746 + 9,839	6,537 + 6,168	5,568 + 1,686	1,732 + 2,681

21.	22.	23.	24.
8,414 + 2,823	7,666 + 6,070	4,843 + 1,932	7,388 + 5,731

1.	**2.**	**3.**	**4.**
5,126	9,636	4,350	3,461
+ 9,732	+ 2,597	+ 7,164	+ 4,148
5.	**6.**	**7.**	**8.**
6,030	5,638	8,896	7,183
+ 5,310	+ 6,359	+ 2,798	+ 2,032
9.	**10.**	**11.**	**12.**
4,267	6,560	9,220	7,710
+ 5,460	+ 5,707	+ 4,149	+ 7,315
13.	**14.**	**15.**	**16.**
8,519	6,441	3,949	6,751
+ 6,187	+ 7,486	+ 6,574	+ 9,016
17.	**18.**	**19.**	**20.**
9,615	4,357	7,107	3,680
+ 3,445	+ 8,996	+ 5,020	+ 9,902
21.	**22.**	**23.**	**24.**
2,466	7,248	8,704	9,092
+ 4,846	+ 4,861	+ 5,537	+ 8,045

ADDITION

1.	2.	3.	4.
5,975 + 8,912	2,488 + 3,096	5,273 + 9,797	2,274 + 8,368

5.	6.	7.	8.
2,067 + 6,598	2,777 + 5,155	6,227 + 7,250	1,978 + 4,238

9.	10.	11.	12.
1,896 + 4,430	5,340 + 7,373	6,707 + 3,138	6,851 + 5,124

13.	14.	15.	16.
8,083 + 3,879	7,666 + 4,193	3,626 + 3,647	9,550 + 6,927

17.	18.	19.	20.
3,684 + 4,321	6,657 + 2,278	5,984 + 7,849	2,986 + 6,403

21.	22.	23.	24.
7,827 + 3,988	2,991 + 9,086	9,742 + 5,682	6,638 + 4,096

SUBTRACTION

1-Digit

1.
```
   9
-  6
____
```

2.
```
   6
-  3
____
```

3.
```
   9
-  2
____
```

4.
```
   9
-  2
____
```

5.
```
   8
-  2
____
```

6.
```
   6
-  5
____
```

7.
```
   2
-  2
____
```

8.
```
   8
-  3
____
```

9.
```
   2
-  1
____
```

10.
```
   6
-  5
____
```

11.
```
   1
-  1
____
```

12.
```
   2
-  1
____
```

13.
```
   9
-  7
____
```

14.
```
   6
-  0
____
```

15.
```
   2
-  0
____
```

16.
```
   8
-  8
____
```

17.
```
   2
-  1
____
```

18.
```
   9
-  8
____
```

19.
```
   7
-  1
____
```

20.
```
   3
-  0
____
```

SUBTRACTION

Answer All the Questions Below:

1. 4 − 4	**2.** 7 − 7	**3.** 4 − 1	**4.** 9 − 8	**5.** 7 − 6
6. 9 − 4	**7.** 5 − 1	**8.** 7 − 6	**9.** 5 − 4	**10.** 8 − 1
11. 7 − 4	**12.** 5 − 0	**13.** 9 − 7	**14.** 3 − 3	**15.** 7 − 1
16. 7 − 6	**17.** 5 − 2	**18.** 8 − 8	**19.** 9 − 0	**20.** 8 − 3

SUBTRACTION

1-Digit

1.	2.	3.	4.	5.
4 − 1	7 − 2	5 − 1	6 − 4	9 − 0

6.	7.	8.	9.	10.
3 − 1	5 − 2	8 − 1	6 − 4	9 − 6

11.	12.	13.	14.	15.
6 − 6	6 − 3	8 − 1	2 − 0	4 − 4

16.	17.	18.	19.	20.
9 − 6	8 − 7	6 − 2	4 − 1	4 − 2

1-Digit | # SUBTRACTION

1.	2.	3.	4.	5.
9 - 2	9 - 1	7 - 7	4 - 2	2 - 1

6.	7.	8.	9.	10.
7 - 2	9 - 3	1 - 1	9 - 4	6 - 5

11.	12.	13.	14.	15.
4 - 1	4 - 4	5 - 1	8 - 7	5 - 2

16.	17.	18.	19.	20.
9 - 3	5 - 2	4 - 2	6 - 1	9 - 4

Answer All the Questions Below:

1. $\begin{array}{r}87\\-\ 27\\\hline\end{array}$	**2.** $\begin{array}{r}86\\-\ 67\\\hline\end{array}$	**3.** $\begin{array}{r}94\\-\ 66\\\hline\end{array}$	**4.** $\begin{array}{r}61\\-\ 43\\\hline\end{array}$	**5.** $\begin{array}{r}89\\-\ 68\\\hline\end{array}$
6. $\begin{array}{r}94\\-\ 59\\\hline\end{array}$	**7.** $\begin{array}{r}79\\-\ 71\\\hline\end{array}$	**8.** $\begin{array}{r}56\\-\ 44\\\hline\end{array}$	**9.** $\begin{array}{r}60\\-\ 46\\\hline\end{array}$	**10.** $\begin{array}{r}82\\-\ 34\\\hline\end{array}$
11. $\begin{array}{r}49\\-\ 11\\\hline\end{array}$	**12.** $\begin{array}{r}41\\-\ 30\\\hline\end{array}$	**13.** $\begin{array}{r}78\\-\ 73\\\hline\end{array}$	**14.** $\begin{array}{r}63\\-\ 40\\\hline\end{array}$	**15.** $\begin{array}{r}99\\-\ 71\\\hline\end{array}$
16. $\begin{array}{r}78\\-\ 22\\\hline\end{array}$	**17.** $\begin{array}{r}91\\-\ 74\\\hline\end{array}$	**18.** $\begin{array}{r}98\\-\ 48\\\hline\end{array}$	**19.** $\begin{array}{r}84\\-\ 51\\\hline\end{array}$	**20.** $\begin{array}{r}73\\-\ 52\\\hline\end{array}$
21. $\begin{array}{r}49\\-\ 13\\\hline\end{array}$	**22.** $\begin{array}{r}64\\-\ 64\\\hline\end{array}$	**23.** $\begin{array}{r}58\\-\ 36\\\hline\end{array}$	**24.** $\begin{array}{r}59\\-\ 50\\\hline\end{array}$	**25.** $\begin{array}{r}58\\-\ 57\\\hline\end{array}$
26. $\begin{array}{r}46\\-\ 31\\\hline\end{array}$	**27.** $\begin{array}{r}96\\-\ 61\\\hline\end{array}$	**28.** $\begin{array}{r}79\\-\ 28\\\hline\end{array}$	**29.** $\begin{array}{r}66\\-\ 30\\\hline\end{array}$	**30.** $\begin{array}{r}95\\-\ 44\\\hline\end{array}$

SUBTRACTION

1.	2.	3.	4.	5.
76 − 12	19 − 15	73 − 46	95 − 41	90 − 21

6.	7.	8.	9.	10.
72 − 17	44 − 42	43 − 20	89 − 41	80 − 22

11.	12.	13.	14.	15.
68 − 52	78 − 69	61 − 34	97 − 54	45 − 41

16.	17.	18.	19.	20.
55 − 29	92 − 34	82 − 68	62 − 26	60 − 30

21.	22.	23.	24.	25.
78 − 63	80 − 34	87 − 28	35 − 28	83 − 65

26.	27.	28.	29.	30.
74 − 36	97 − 60	80 − 14	89 − 42	81 − 16

SUBTRACTION

2-Digit

1.	2.	3.	4.	5.
72 − 53	53 − 43	91 − 73	25 − 12	43 − 28

6.	7.	8.	9.	10.
70 − 43	69 − 22	31 − 23	66 − 25	81 − 53

11.	12.	13.	14.	15.
92 − 63	84 − 29	58 − 49	67 − 18	66 − 53

16.	17.	18.	19.	20.
35 − 17	77 − 59	97 − 90	51 − 35	22 − 11

21.	22.	23.	24.	25.
86 − 54	58 − 22	84 − 19	84 − 28	98 − 96

26.	27.	28.	29.	30.
79 − 52	66 − 13	31 − 16	91 − 75	63 − 10

SUBTRACTION

2-Digit

Answer All the Questions Below:

1. 63 − 21	**2.** 74 − 68	**3.** 32 − 28	**4.** 96 − 92	**5.** 66 − 14
6. 70 − 33	**7.** 84 − 69	**8.** 68 − 19	**9.** 34 − 31	**10.** 80 − 76
11. 84 − 66	**12.** 81 − 56	**13.** 43 − 31	**14.** 77 − 20	**15.** 84 − 15
16. 38 − 15	**17.** 67 − 33	**18.** 57 − 14	**19.** 72 − 56	**20.** 74 − 52
21. 56 − 33	**22.** 95 − 79	**23.** 48 − 34	**24.** 69 − 37	**25.** 90 − 22
26. 66 − 51	**27.** 92 − 76	**28.** 75 − 29	**29.** 46 − 45	**30.** 56 − 36

Answer All the Questions Below:

1. 71 - 68	2. 98 - 42	3. 89 - 77	4. 89 - 88	5. 67 - 37
6. 66 - 30	7. 86 - 32	8. 57 - 46	9. 77 - 39	10. 79 - 69
11. 41 - 30	12. 81 - 48	13. 91 - 61	14. 63 - 17	15. 83 - 46
16. 66 - 12	17. 70 - 51	18. 55 - 37	19. 98 - 78	20. 35 - 19
21. 63 - 29	22. 83 - 46	23. 77 - 38	24. 51 - 41	25. 90 - 24
26. 56 - 50	27. 34 - 25	28. 92 - 38	29. 72 - 28	30. 92 - 75

SUBTRACTION

1. 216 − 188	**2.** 445 − 142	**3.** 676 − 615	**4.** 690 − 460	**5.** 729 − 420
6. 868 − 132	**7.** 470 − 241	**8.** 975 − 118	**9.** 298 − 161	**10.** 925 − 245
11. 750 − 619	**12.** 735 − 207	**13.** 529 − 505	**14.** 698 − 656	**15.** 299 − 226
16. 892 − 397	**17.** 917 − 882	**18.** 314 − 252	**19.** 972 − 310	**20.** 665 − 196
21. 993 − 832	**22.** 906 − 445	**23.** 726 − 619	**24.** 864 − 782	**25.** 568 − 446
26. 618 − 394	**27.** 617 − 450	**28.** 967 − 883	**29.** 588 − 495	**30.** 602 − 329

SUBTRACTION

3-Digit

Answer All the Questions Below:

1. 683 − 111	**2.** 905 − 324	**3.** 226 − 176	**4.** 724 − 343	**5.** 440 − 409
6. 364 − 195	**7.** 906 − 744	**8.** 987 − 378	**9.** 288 − 122	**10.** 932 − 629
11. 926 − 317	**12.** 212 − 119	**13.** 241 − 229	**14.** 709 − 165	**15.** 571 − 173
16. 707 − 111	**17.** 377 − 311	**18.** 401 − 328	**19.** 576 − 329	**20.** 701 − 274
21. 812 − 201	**22.** 798 − 628	**23.** 484 − 252	**24.** 676 − 143	**25.** 744 − 324
26. 855 − 586	**27.** 968 − 282	**28.** 705 − 304	**29.** 620 − 331	**30.** 415 − 117

Answer All the Questions Below:

1.	2.	3.	4.	5.
665 - 522	791 - 175	950 - 943	785 - 492	582 - 128

6.	7.	8.	9.	10.
860 - 527	936 - 223	936 - 267	945 - 623	433 - 384

11.	12.	13.	14.	15.
781 - 567	913 - 496	337 - 199	553 - 489	342 - 279

16.	17.	18.	19.	20.
834 - 780	969 - 403	893 - 675	706 - 621	521 - 163

21.	22.	23.	24.	25.
837 - 391	774 - 210	768 - 603	676 - 646	614 - 508

26.	27.	28.	29.	30.
653 - 360	773 - 264	667 - 505	423 - 198	670 - 439

SUBTRACTION

Answer All the Questions Below:

1. 944 − 815	**2.** 676 − 450	**3.** 968 − 280	**4.** 724 − 148	**5.** 423 − 355
6. 323 − 293	**7.** 898 − 593	**8.** 553 − 523	**9.** 409 − 135	**10.** 957 − 170
11. 816 − 410	**12.** 189 − 125	**13.** 577 − 134	**14.** 993 − 166	**15.** 854 − 450
16. 510 − 223	**17.** 574 − 532	**18.** 509 − 327	**19.** 558 − 184	**20.** 674 − 578
21. 793 − 355	**22.** 961 − 930	**23.** 979 − 334	**24.** 777 − 352	**25.** 982 − 609
26. 746 − 540	**27.** 315 − 277	**28.** 130 − 111	**29.** 918 − 527	**30.** 885 − 839

SUBTRACTION

1.	2.	3.	4.	5.
404 − 234	389 − 307	828 − 695	924 − 539	580 − 158

6.	7.	8.	9.	10.
606 − 355	782 − 775	992 − 319	793 − 518	609 − 437

11.	12.	13.	14.	15.
265 − 191	926 − 339	764 − 372	629 − 412	589 − 582

16.	17.	18.	19.	20.
475 − 270	289 − 216	396 − 188	940 − 737	981 − 889

21.	22.	23.	24.	25.
845 − 261	661 − 602	930 − 234	795 − 347	921 − 659

26.	27.	28.	29.	30.
646 − 455	850 − 354	535 − 138	431 − 183	490 − 421

SUBTRACTION

4-Digit

1. 9,941 − 6,578	**2.** 6,787 − 5,349	**3.** 9,940 − 5,593	**4.** 9,590 − 4,049
5. 5,078 − 3,430	**6.** 3,474 − 3,073	**7.** 9,881 − 9,336	**8.** 7,659 − 5,253
9. 9,541 − 5,171	**10.** 7,524 − 2,960	**11.** 8,015 − 3,677	**12.** 8,429 − 4,751
13. 7,440 − 5,988	**14.** 5,038 − 4,832	**15.** 7,113 − 4,955	**16.** 3,665 − 3,444
17. 7,230 − 4,937	**18.** 3,825 − 2,125	**19.** 7,691 − 3,420	**20.** 4,709 − 3,549
21. 9,110 − 7,625	**22.** 6,718 − 4,361	**23.** 7,965 − 4,652	**24.** 7,619 − 5,475

SUBTRACTION

4-Digit

Answer All the Questions Below:

1. 8,545 − 3,388	**2.** 6,407 − 3,726	**3.** 8,943 − 5,987	**4.** 7,487 − 5,320
5. 7,960 − 3,058	**6.** 6,220 − 4,948	**7.** 8,148 − 6,584	**8.** 7,859 − 6,415
9. 8,930 − 8,743	**10.** 5,673 − 3,709	**11.** 8,950 − 4,974	**12.** 5,922 − 4,096
13. 9,197 − 3,221	**14.** 6,013 − 4,366	**15.** 4,167 − 2,304	**16.** 7,586 − 2,346
17. 8,486 − 7,282	**18.** 5,582 − 4,723	**19.** 6,582 − 2,766	**20.** 7,949 − 7,246
21. 8,379 − 4,754	**22.** 7,546 − 4,943	**23.** 9,270 − 6,966	**24.** 6,773 − 5,425

SUBTRACTION

4-Digit

Answer All the Questions Below:

1. 7,843 − 6,387	**2.** 7,135 − 2,178	**3.** 9,620 − 8,212	**4.** 9,021 − 3,323
5. 5,020 − 2,161	**6.** 8,443 − 7,400	**7.** 6,520 − 6,427	**8.** 9,740 − 7,667
9. 6,766 − 4,457	**10.** 6,563 − 6,316	**11.** 3,458 − 2,742	**12.** 7,892 − 3,160
13. 8,756 − 3,162	**14.** 7,357 − 4,849	**15.** 7,914 − 7,274	**16.** 8,143 − 4,850
17. 8,297 − 8,105	**18.** 7,751 − 4,708	**19.** 9,200 − 8,524	**20.** 8,426 − 7,281
21. 7,302 − 4,846	**22.** 8,830 − 5,019	**23.** 8,319 − 6,586	**24.** 8,669 − 7,072

Answer All the Questions Below:

1.	2.	3.	4.
8,812 − 4,816	6,731 − 4,003	7,687 − 6,213	6,329 − 4,154

5.	6.	7.	8.
9,064 − 6,892	9,852 − 9,294	7,114 − 3,996	8,081 − 4,034

9.	10.	11.	12.
7,221 − 3,531	9,586 − 3,755	8,786 − 7,406	6,398 − 5,818

13.	14.	15.	16.
6,800 − 5,174	6,977 − 3,629	7,233 − 6,879	8,419 − 2,229

17.	18.	19.	20.
8,648 − 6,023	4,546 − 3,610	7,070 − 6,420	7,466 − 6,250

21.	22.	23.	24.
8,251 − 3,434	6,992 − 6,103	7,880 − 5,275	9,887 − 9,528

SUBTRACTION

4-Digit

1.	2.	3.	4.
7,251 − 3,532	6,679 − 2,899	9,106 − 6,918	8,082 − 2,562

5.	6.	7.	8.
9,983 − 5,137	4,928 − 2,461	6,480 − 3,735	6,661 − 4,125

9.	10.	11.	12.
5,683 − 5,242	9,727 − 2,635	4,713 − 2,675	9,818 − 2,286

13.	14.	15.	16.
5,554 − 2,736	9,044 − 4,196	9,040 − 8,810	9,819 − 2,398

17.	18.	19.	20.
6,990 − 3,827	9,161 − 7,510	9,495 − 2,249	7,987 − 7,131

21.	22.	23.	24.
5,223 − 5,216	7,226 − 3,927	9,552 − 8,759	3,021 − 2,777

Answer All the Questions Below:

1.
$$\begin{array}{r} 2 \\ \times\ 2 \\ \hline \end{array}$$

2.
$$\begin{array}{r} 8 \\ \times\ 1 \\ \hline \end{array}$$

3.
$$\begin{array}{r} 6 \\ \times\ 1 \\ \hline \end{array}$$

4.
$$\begin{array}{r} 9 \\ \times\ 1 \\ \hline \end{array}$$

5.
$$\begin{array}{r} 8 \\ \times\ 7 \\ \hline \end{array}$$

6.
$$\begin{array}{r} 6 \\ \times\ 5 \\ \hline \end{array}$$

7.
$$\begin{array}{r} 7 \\ \times\ 1 \\ \hline \end{array}$$

8.
$$\begin{array}{r} 6 \\ \times\ 5 \\ \hline \end{array}$$

9.
$$\begin{array}{r} 3 \\ \times\ 7 \\ \hline \end{array}$$

10.
$$\begin{array}{r} 6 \\ \times\ 1 \\ \hline \end{array}$$

11.
$$\begin{array}{r} 9 \\ \times\ 8 \\ \hline \end{array}$$

12.
$$\begin{array}{r} 7 \\ \times\ 4 \\ \hline \end{array}$$

13.
$$\begin{array}{r} 7 \\ \times\ 7 \\ \hline \end{array}$$

14.
$$\begin{array}{r} 3 \\ \times\ 1 \\ \hline \end{array}$$

15.
$$\begin{array}{r} 2 \\ \times\ 8 \\ \hline \end{array}$$

16.
$$\begin{array}{r} 7 \\ \times\ 2 \\ \hline \end{array}$$

17.
$$\begin{array}{r} 5 \\ \times\ 1 \\ \hline \end{array}$$

18.
$$\begin{array}{r} 3 \\ \times\ 6 \\ \hline \end{array}$$

19.
$$\begin{array}{r} 2 \\ \times\ 9 \\ \hline \end{array}$$

20.
$$\begin{array}{r} 2 \\ \times\ 1 \\ \hline \end{array}$$

Answer All the Questions Below:

1.	2.	3.	4.	5.
1 × 4	5 × 7	1 × 8	4 × 5	3 × 5

6.	7.	8.	9.	10.
5 × 1	8 × 9	1 × 1	5 × 5	2 × 3

11.	12.	13.	14.	15.
5 × 8	5 × 3	1 × 9	6 × 1	3 × 8

16.	17.	18.	19.	20.
6 × 8	1 × 1	3 × 4	4 × 9	7 × 1

MULTIPLICATION

1-Digit

Answer All the Questions Below:

1. $\begin{array}{r} 8 \\ \times\ 8 \\ \hline \end{array}$	2. $\begin{array}{r} 6 \\ \times\ 8 \\ \hline \end{array}$	3. $\begin{array}{r} 2 \\ \times\ 1 \\ \hline \end{array}$	4. $\begin{array}{r} 9 \\ \times\ 7 \\ \hline \end{array}$	5. $\begin{array}{r} 1 \\ \times\ 2 \\ \hline \end{array}$
6. $\begin{array}{r} 9 \\ \times\ 4 \\ \hline \end{array}$	7. $\begin{array}{r} 6 \\ \times\ 6 \\ \hline \end{array}$	8. $\begin{array}{r} 2 \\ \times\ 9 \\ \hline \end{array}$	9. $\begin{array}{r} 9 \\ \times\ 4 \\ \hline \end{array}$	10. $\begin{array}{r} 1 \\ \times\ 1 \\ \hline \end{array}$
11. $\begin{array}{r} 6 \\ \times\ 5 \\ \hline \end{array}$	12. $\begin{array}{r} 9 \\ \times\ 1 \\ \hline \end{array}$	13. $\begin{array}{r} 8 \\ \times\ 8 \\ \hline \end{array}$	14. $\begin{array}{r} 3 \\ \times\ 9 \\ \hline \end{array}$	15. $\begin{array}{r} 2 \\ \times\ 5 \\ \hline \end{array}$
16. $\begin{array}{r} 9 \\ \times\ 9 \\ \hline \end{array}$	17. $\begin{array}{r} 1 \\ \times\ 6 \\ \hline \end{array}$	18. $\begin{array}{r} 7 \\ \times\ 7 \\ \hline \end{array}$	19. $\begin{array}{r} 5 \\ \times\ 7 \\ \hline \end{array}$	20. $\begin{array}{r} 8 \\ \times\ 9 \\ \hline \end{array}$

Answer All the Questions Below:

1.	2.	3.	4.	5.
8 × 7	9 × 1	8 × 7	6 × 5	8 × 5

6.	7.	8.	9.	10.
9 × 6	4 × 1	9 × 9	8 × 5	4 × 3

11.	12.	13.	14.	15.
9 × 1	1 × 3	9 × 7	1 × 7	3 × 8

16.	17.	18.	19.	20.
1 × 1	7 × 8	2 × 7	6 × 7	9 × 1

2-Digit MULTIPLICATION

1. $\begin{array}{r} 69 \\ \times\ 97 \\ \hline \end{array}$	**2.** $\begin{array}{r} 56 \\ \times\ 57 \\ \hline \end{array}$	**3.** $\begin{array}{r} 11 \\ \times\ 30 \\ \hline \end{array}$	**4.** $\begin{array}{r} 75 \\ \times\ 75 \\ \hline \end{array}$	**5.** $\begin{array}{r} 22 \\ \times\ 46 \\ \hline \end{array}$
6. $\begin{array}{r} 45 \\ \times\ 61 \\ \hline \end{array}$	**7.** $\begin{array}{r} 53 \\ \times\ 46 \\ \hline \end{array}$	**8.** $\begin{array}{r} 23 \\ \times\ 65 \\ \hline \end{array}$	**9.** $\begin{array}{r} 50 \\ \times\ 10 \\ \hline \end{array}$	**10.** $\begin{array}{r} 45 \\ \times\ 55 \\ \hline \end{array}$
11. $\begin{array}{r} 76 \\ \times\ 85 \\ \hline \end{array}$	**12.** $\begin{array}{r} 52 \\ \times\ 76 \\ \hline \end{array}$	**13.** $\begin{array}{r} 80 \\ \times\ 63 \\ \hline \end{array}$	**14.** $\begin{array}{r} 85 \\ \times\ 25 \\ \hline \end{array}$	**15.** $\begin{array}{r} 67 \\ \times\ 36 \\ \hline \end{array}$
16. $\begin{array}{r} 85 \\ \times\ 82 \\ \hline \end{array}$	**17.** $\begin{array}{r} 79 \\ \times\ 69 \\ \hline \end{array}$	**18.** $\begin{array}{r} 59 \\ \times\ 73 \\ \hline \end{array}$	**19.** $\begin{array}{r} 53 \\ \times\ 28 \\ \hline \end{array}$	**20.** $\begin{array}{r} 69 \\ \times\ 77 \\ \hline \end{array}$
21. $\begin{array}{r} 69 \\ \times\ 31 \\ \hline \end{array}$	**22.** $\begin{array}{r} 83 \\ \times\ 38 \\ \hline \end{array}$	**23.** $\begin{array}{r} 58 \\ \times\ 81 \\ \hline \end{array}$	**24.** $\begin{array}{r} 26 \\ \times\ 81 \\ \hline \end{array}$	**25.** $\begin{array}{r} 82 \\ \times\ 73 \\ \hline \end{array}$
26. $\begin{array}{r} 67 \\ \times\ 17 \\ \hline \end{array}$	**27.** $\begin{array}{r} 75 \\ \times\ 93 \\ \hline \end{array}$	**28.** $\begin{array}{r} 42 \\ \times\ 55 \\ \hline \end{array}$	**29.** $\begin{array}{r} 79 \\ \times\ 66 \\ \hline \end{array}$	**30.** $\begin{array}{r} 38 \\ \times\ 97 \\ \hline \end{array}$

2-Digit MULTIPLICATION

1. 60 × 41	**2.** 71 × 33	**3.** 31 × 88	**4.** 44 × 75	**5.** 49 × 42
6. 11 × 73	**7.** 61 × 67	**8.** 13 × 23	**9.** 50 × 17	**10.** 11 × 30
11. 18 × 39	**12.** 32 × 21	**13.** 16 × 57	**14.** 66 × 37	**15.** 47 × 79
16. 61 × 69	**17.** 44 × 50	**18.** 69 × 16	**19.** 34 × 76	**20.** 34 × 77
21. 98 × 69	**22.** 17 × 97	**23.** 41 × 24	**24.** 78 × 57	**25.** 51 × 23
26. 41 × 60	**27.** 82 × 53	**28.** 37 × 40	**29.** 16 × 27	**30.** 27 × 44

MULTIPLICATION

2-Digit

1.
$$65 \times 85$$

2.
$$41 \times 62$$

3.
$$88 \times 12$$

4.
$$68 \times 29$$

5.
$$21 \times 34$$

6.
$$60 \times 47$$

7.
$$15 \times 15$$

8.
$$39 \times 80$$

9.
$$43 \times 12$$

10.
$$65 \times 80$$

11.
$$24 \times 82$$

12.
$$33 \times 50$$

13.
$$44 \times 76$$

14.
$$68 \times 22$$

15.
$$11 \times 62$$

16.
$$98 \times 15$$

17.
$$13 \times 78$$

18.
$$89 \times 12$$

19.
$$22 \times 21$$

20.
$$57 \times 97$$

21.
$$43 \times 96$$

22.
$$94 \times 42$$

23.
$$16 \times 88$$

24.
$$99 \times 64$$

25.
$$45 \times 27$$

26.
$$81 \times 55$$

27.
$$60 \times 25$$

28.
$$97 \times 81$$

29.
$$74 \times 15$$

30.
$$40 \times 84$$

MULTIPLICATION

2-Digit

Answer All the Questions Below:

1. $\begin{array}{r} 71 \\ \times\ 37 \\ \hline \end{array}$	**2.** $\begin{array}{r} 32 \\ \times\ 55 \\ \hline \end{array}$	**3.** $\begin{array}{r} 19 \\ \times\ 41 \\ \hline \end{array}$	**4.** $\begin{array}{r} 94 \\ \times\ 23 \\ \hline \end{array}$	**5.** $\begin{array}{r} 49 \\ \times\ 93 \\ \hline \end{array}$
6. $\begin{array}{r} 69 \\ \times\ 89 \\ \hline \end{array}$	**7.** $\begin{array}{r} 68 \\ \times\ 40 \\ \hline \end{array}$	**8.** $\begin{array}{r} 20 \\ \times\ 39 \\ \hline \end{array}$	**9.** $\begin{array}{r} 53 \\ \times\ 86 \\ \hline \end{array}$	**10.** $\begin{array}{r} 19 \\ \times\ 46 \\ \hline \end{array}$
11. $\begin{array}{r} 14 \\ \times\ 44 \\ \hline \end{array}$	**12.** $\begin{array}{r} 43 \\ \times\ 78 \\ \hline \end{array}$	**13.** $\begin{array}{r} 56 \\ \times\ 10 \\ \hline \end{array}$	**14.** $\begin{array}{r} 52 \\ \times\ 29 \\ \hline \end{array}$	**15.** $\begin{array}{r} 37 \\ \times\ 31 \\ \hline \end{array}$
16. $\begin{array}{r} 65 \\ \times\ 19 \\ \hline \end{array}$	**17.** $\begin{array}{r} 68 \\ \times\ 55 \\ \hline \end{array}$	**18.** $\begin{array}{r} 54 \\ \times\ 58 \\ \hline \end{array}$	**19.** $\begin{array}{r} 97 \\ \times\ 67 \\ \hline \end{array}$	**20.** $\begin{array}{r} 97 \\ \times\ 24 \\ \hline \end{array}$
21. $\begin{array}{r} 70 \\ \times\ 40 \\ \hline \end{array}$	**22.** $\begin{array}{r} 79 \\ \times\ 85 \\ \hline \end{array}$	**23.** $\begin{array}{r} 97 \\ \times\ 98 \\ \hline \end{array}$	**24.** $\begin{array}{r} 54 \\ \times\ 65 \\ \hline \end{array}$	**25.** $\begin{array}{r} 36 \\ \times\ 51 \\ \hline \end{array}$
26. $\begin{array}{r} 99 \\ \times\ 71 \\ \hline \end{array}$	**27.** $\begin{array}{r} 45 \\ \times\ 24 \\ \hline \end{array}$	**28.** $\begin{array}{r} 37 \\ \times\ 51 \\ \hline \end{array}$	**29.** $\begin{array}{r} 54 \\ \times\ 23 \\ \hline \end{array}$	**30.** $\begin{array}{r} 78 \\ \times\ 88 \\ \hline \end{array}$

2-Digit MULTIPLICATION

1. $\begin{array}{r} 99 \\ \times\ 33 \\ \hline \end{array}$	**2.** $\begin{array}{r} 79 \\ \times\ 48 \\ \hline \end{array}$	**3.** $\begin{array}{r} 82 \\ \times\ 74 \\ \hline \end{array}$	**4.** $\begin{array}{r} 71 \\ \times\ 90 \\ \hline \end{array}$	**5.** $\begin{array}{r} 55 \\ \times\ 14 \\ \hline \end{array}$
6. $\begin{array}{r} 19 \\ \times\ 51 \\ \hline \end{array}$	**7.** $\begin{array}{r} 94 \\ \times\ 14 \\ \hline \end{array}$	**8.** $\begin{array}{r} 36 \\ \times\ 44 \\ \hline \end{array}$	**9.** $\begin{array}{r} 52 \\ \times\ 31 \\ \hline \end{array}$	**10.** $\begin{array}{r} 21 \\ \times\ 24 \\ \hline \end{array}$
11. $\begin{array}{r} 87 \\ \times\ 25 \\ \hline \end{array}$	**12.** $\begin{array}{r} 49 \\ \times\ 44 \\ \hline \end{array}$	**13.** $\begin{array}{r} 62 \\ \times\ 20 \\ \hline \end{array}$	**14.** $\begin{array}{r} 67 \\ \times\ 53 \\ \hline \end{array}$	**15.** $\begin{array}{r} 15 \\ \times\ 38 \\ \hline \end{array}$
16. $\begin{array}{r} 88 \\ \times\ 50 \\ \hline \end{array}$	**17.** $\begin{array}{r} 11 \\ \times\ 68 \\ \hline \end{array}$	**18.** $\begin{array}{r} 67 \\ \times\ 87 \\ \hline \end{array}$	**19.** $\begin{array}{r} 58 \\ \times\ 59 \\ \hline \end{array}$	**20.** $\begin{array}{r} 33 \\ \times\ 73 \\ \hline \end{array}$
21. $\begin{array}{r} 99 \\ \times\ 35 \\ \hline \end{array}$	**22.** $\begin{array}{r} 38 \\ \times\ 53 \\ \hline \end{array}$	**23.** $\begin{array}{r} 37 \\ \times\ 50 \\ \hline \end{array}$	**24.** $\begin{array}{r} 23 \\ \times\ 16 \\ \hline \end{array}$	**25.** $\begin{array}{r} 27 \\ \times\ 42 \\ \hline \end{array}$
26. $\begin{array}{r} 77 \\ \times\ 61 \\ \hline \end{array}$	**27.** $\begin{array}{r} 90 \\ \times\ 49 \\ \hline \end{array}$	**28.** $\begin{array}{r} 19 \\ \times\ 72 \\ \hline \end{array}$	**29.** $\begin{array}{r} 27 \\ \times\ 41 \\ \hline \end{array}$	**30.** $\begin{array}{r} 50 \\ \times\ 52 \\ \hline \end{array}$

MULTIPLICATION

3-Digit

1. 417 × 6	**2.** 679 × 10	**3.** 344 × 27	**4.** 548 × 6	**5.** 844 × 11
6. 278 × 8	**7.** 437 × 1	**8.** 586 × 10	**9.** 384 × 21	**10.** 806 × 12
11. 271 × 29	**12.** 231 × 21	**13.** 274 × 20	**14.** 387 × 25	**15.** 386 × 21
16. 316 × 12	**17.** 649 × 10	**18.** 135 × 67	**19.** 793 × 1	**20.** 125 × 30
21. 227 × 23	**22.** 122 × 56	**23.** 255 × 3	**24.** 374 × 13	**25.** 811 × 2
26. 589 × 11	**27.** 457 × 5	**28.** 621 × 11	**29.** 769 × 6	**30.** 146 × 17

Answer All the Questions Below:

1.
$$140 \times 51$$

2.
$$566 \times 13$$

3.
$$111 \times 77$$

4.
$$288 \times 24$$

5.
$$672 \times 10$$

6.
$$224 \times 26$$

7.
$$125 \times 55$$

8.
$$196 \times 33$$

9.
$$203 \times 4$$

10.
$$803 \times 4$$

11.
$$510 \times 15$$

12.
$$323 \times 18$$

13.
$$161 \times 13$$

14.
$$678 \times 11$$

15.
$$118 \times 7$$

16.
$$424 \times 7$$

17.
$$817 \times 12$$

18.
$$588 \times 15$$

19.
$$513 \times 15$$

20.
$$998 \times 7$$

21.
$$567 \times 4$$

22.
$$497 \times 14$$

23.
$$929 \times 7$$

24.
$$676 \times 10$$

25.
$$312 \times 30$$

26.
$$132 \times 29$$

27.
$$717 \times 2$$

28.
$$448 \times 22$$

29.
$$780 \times 6$$

30.
$$224 \times 10$$

Answer All the Questions Below:

1. 638×10	**2.** 111×22	**3.** 150×28	**4.** 268×23	**5.** 285×3
6. 477×7	**7.** 519×7	**8.** 266×1	**9.** 150×58	**10.** 252×21
11. 331×6	**12.** 426×12	**13.** 236×20	**14.** 158×3	**15.** 144×20
16. 276×2	**17.** 706×6	**18.** 203×15	**19.** 331×11	**20.** 563×14
21. 130×6	**22.** 488×4	**23.** 979×4	**24.** 582×2	**25.** 205×6
26. 175×17	**27.** 156×42	**28.** 443×6	**29.** 123×69	**30.** 256×22

Answer All the Questions Below:

1.
461
× 9

2.
172
× 47

3.
320
× 7

4.
183
× 44

5.
129
× 72

6.
437
× 21

7.
434
× 4

8.
699
× 6

9.
145
× 17

10.
216
× 43

11.
248
× 19

12.
193
× 6

13.
145
× 52

14.
208
× 29

15.
772
× 3

16.
163
× 19

17.
175
× 56

18.
217
× 33

19.
201
× 8

20.
133
× 26

21.
230
× 17

22.
848
× 2

23.
220
× 25

24.
552
× 3

25.
120
× 70

26.
448
× 1

27.
389
× 21

28.
473
× 13

29.
186
× 38

30.
906
× 6

Answer All the Questions Below:

1. 353×15	**2.** 203×24	**3.** 253×12	**4.** 725×5	**5.** 140×34
6. 257×17	**7.** 242×27	**8.** 236×12	**9.** 465×10	**10.** 386×8
11. 733×9	**12.** 258×1	**13.** 834×7	**14.** 193×43	**15.** 400×7
16. 568×2	**17.** 176×14	**18.** 597×5	**19.** 683×13	**20.** 405×9
21. 146×46	**22.** 237×22	**23.** 145×13	**24.** 589×10	**25.** 334×7
26. 816×5	**27.** 158×39	**28.** 809×1	**29.** 133×10	**30.** 679×13

MULTIPLICATION

4-Digit

Answer All the Questions Below:

1. 5,621 × 92	**2.** 8,211 × 83	**3.** 2,769 × 98	**4.** 2,567 × 45
5. 4,782 × 75	**6.** 8,796 × 79	**7.** 5,981 × 67	**8.** 4,238 × 60
9. 5,592 × 69	**10.** 4,291 × 15	**11.** 7,822 × 61	**12.** 9,684 × 71
13. 4,059 × 88	**14.** 9,876 × 59	**15.** 2,100 × 42	**16.** 5,515 × 35
17. 9,277 × 91	**18.** 2,277 × 49	**19.** 4,293 × 16	**20.** 3,428 × 90
21. 3,859 × 37	**22.** 6,769 × 68	**23.** 4,161 × 78	**24.** 9,332 × 92

MULTIPLICATION

4-Digit

1.
$$9{,}817 \times 20$$

2.
$$9{,}487 \times 42$$

3.
$$8{,}943 \times 65$$

4.
$$1{,}758 \times 59$$

5.
$$7{,}077 \times 86$$

6.
$$5{,}130 \times 50$$

7.
$$7{,}641 \times 39$$

8.
$$4{,}916 \times 48$$

9.
$$3{,}973 \times 26$$

10.
$$7{,}761 \times 88$$

11.
$$6{,}852 \times 38$$

12.
$$5{,}100 \times 49$$

13.
$$7{,}833 \times 25$$

14.
$$7{,}193 \times 63$$

15.
$$2{,}931 \times 91$$

16.
$$5{,}035 \times 55$$

17.
$$4{,}827 \times 49$$

18.
$$5{,}726 \times 19$$

19.
$$9{,}405 \times 35$$

20.
$$7{,}781 \times 42$$

21.
$$9{,}745 \times 41$$

22.
$$4{,}108 \times 62$$

23.
$$5{,}268 \times 82$$

24.
$$7{,}627 \times 78$$

4-Digit MULTIPLICATION

1. 2,722 × 13	**2.** 8,845 × 11	**3.** 6,764 × 19	**4.** 4,313 × 88
5. 9,689 × 14	**6.** 4,835 × 41	**7.** 3,558 × 29	**8.** 5,430 × 99
9. 5,545 × 89	**10.** 5,841 × 32	**11.** 2,737 × 76	**12.** 9,196 × 39
13. 3,373 × 73	**14.** 5,164 × 50	**15.** 6,949 × 30	**16.** 3,777 × 34
17. 1,717 × 67	**18.** 2,362 × 75	**19.** 3,067 × 88	**20.** 3,479 × 19
21. 8,804 × 79	**22.** 6,923 × 53	**23.** 7,629 × 90	**24.** 8,346 × 20

MULTIPLICATION

4-Digit

Answer All the Questions Below:

1. 4,407 × 97	**2.** 6,827 × 53	**3.** 4,052 × 50	**4.** 5,752 × 83
5. 2,852 × 76	**6.** 4,731 × 33	**7.** 4,804 × 78	**8.** 4,828 × 52
9. 4,922 × 92	**10.** 7,007 × 11	**11.** 5,229 × 52	**12.** 8,156 × 77
13. 8,777 × 47	**14.** 2,945 × 79	**15.** 2,330 × 19	**16.** 9,889 × 62
17. 3,402 × 18	**18.** 3,592 × 73	**19.** 6,321 × 84	**20.** 2,835 × 12
21. 7,388 × 37	**22.** 3,436 × 10	**23.** 6,203 × 92	**24.** 3,187 × 88

MULTIPLICATION

4-Digit

1.
$$2{,}067 \times 99$$

2.
$$4{,}067 \times 77$$

3.
$$7{,}344 \times 78$$

4.
$$2{,}945 \times 43$$

5.
$$6{,}148 \times 28$$

6.
$$3{,}352 \times 93$$

7.
$$2{,}938 \times 94$$

8.
$$4{,}957 \times 24$$

9.
$$3{,}443 \times 30$$

10.
$$2{,}247 \times 26$$

11.
$$9{,}043 \times 41$$

12.
$$4{,}846 \times 61$$

13.
$$6{,}723 \times 62$$

14.
$$1{,}876 \times 40$$

15.
$$8{,}795 \times 42$$

16.
$$2{,}539 \times 99$$

17.
$$2{,}696 \times 33$$

18.
$$4{,}538 \times 83$$

19.
$$4{,}767 \times 73$$

20.
$$2{,}914 \times 24$$

21.
$$5{,}146 \times 84$$

22.
$$2{,}166 \times 49$$

23.
$$4{,}976 \times 32$$

24.
$$5{,}318 \times 72$$

1-Digit

DIVISION

Answer All the Questions Below:

1.
$$6 \div 1 =$$

2.
$$9 \div 9 =$$

3.
$$10 \div 2 =$$

4.
$$5 \div 5 =$$

5.
$$7 \div 7 =$$

6.
$$14 \div 2 =$$

7.
$$18 \div 6 =$$

8.
$$6 \div 3 =$$

9.
$$8 \div 2 =$$

10.
$$14 \div 2 =$$

11.
$$8 \div 8 =$$

12.
$$12 \div 2 =$$

13.
$$15 \div 5 =$$

14.
$$9 \div 9 =$$

15.
$$16 \div 4 =$$

16.
$$7 \div 7 =$$

17.
$$12 \div 2 =$$

18.
$$20 \div 4 =$$

19.
$$7 \div 7 =$$

20.
$$12 \div 3 =$$

Answer All the Questions Below:

1.   15 ÷ 5 = ______

2.   8 ÷ 2 = ______

3.   16 ÷ 4 = ______

4.   20 ÷ 4 = ______

5.   12 ÷ 2 = ______

6.   20 ÷ 1 = ______

7.   18 ÷ 2 = ______

8.   6 ÷ 1 = ______

9.   14 ÷ 2 = ______

10.   12 ÷ 6 = ______

11.   8 ÷ 4 = ______

12.   12 ÷ 6 = ______

13.   1 ÷ 1 = ______

14.   3 ÷ 3 = ______

15.   5 ÷ 1 = ______

16.   17 ÷ 1 = ______

17.   16 ÷ 8 = ______

18.   7 ÷ 7 = ______

19.   13 ÷ 1 = ______

20.   12 ÷ 3 = ______

Answer All the Questions Below:

1.
$$8 \div 8$$

2.
$$9 \div 9$$

3.
$$18 \div 9$$

4.
$$7 \div 7$$

5.
$$16 \div 8$$

6.
$$14 \div 7$$

7.
$$12 \div 6$$

8.
$$7 \div 7$$

9.
$$11 \div 1$$

10.
$$18 \div 2$$

11.
$$6 \div 1$$

12.
$$10 \div 5$$

13.
$$10 \div 5$$

14.
$$15 \div 5$$

15.
$$9 \div 3$$

16.
$$12 \div 3$$

17.
$$15 \div 5$$

18.
$$12 \div 4$$

19.
$$14 \div 7$$

20.
$$6 \div 3$$

Answer All the Questions Below:

1. 15 ÷ 3 =

2. 8 ÷ 8 =

3. 7 ÷ 7 =

4. 12 ÷ 4 =

5. 10 ÷ 5 =

6. 4 ÷ 2 =

7. 12 ÷ 3 =

8. 15 ÷ 1 =

9. 11 ÷ 1 =

10. 7 ÷ 7 =

11. 8 ÷ 8 =

12. 15 ÷ 5 =

13. 18 ÷ 1 =

14. 10 ÷ 5 =

15. 6 ÷ 6 =

16. 16 ÷ 8 =

17. 6 ÷ 6 =

18. 10 ÷ 2 =

19. 5 ÷ 1 =

20. 15 ÷ 3 =

2-Digit

Answer All the Questions Below:

1. $34 \div 2$	**2.** $74 \div 1$	**3.** $18 \div 9$	**4.** $87 \div 1$	**5.** $84 \div 6$
6. $77 \div 7$	**7.** $84 \div 6$	**8.** $52 \div 2$	**9.** $81 \div 9$	**10.** $88 \div 8$
11. $36 \div 6$	**12.** $18 \div 6$	**13.** $48 \div 6$	**14.** $63 \div 7$	**15.** $63 \div 9$
16. $49 \div 7$	**17.** $28 \div 7$	**18.** $24 \div 6$	**19.** $36 \div 6$	**20.** $40 \div 8$
21. $60 \div 3$	**22.** $28 \div 2$	**23.** $86 \div 2$	**24.** $18 \div 9$	**25.** $36 \div 9$
26. $54 \div 3$	**27.** $45 \div 9$	**28.** $95 \div 5$	**29.** $40 \div 5$	**30.** $40 \div 8$

Answer All the Questions Below:

1. $56 \div 8$	**2.** $84 \div 4$	**3.** $57 \div 1$	**4.** $32 \div 8$	**5.** $60 \div 4$
6. $81 \div 1$	**7.** $57 \div 3$	**8.** $16 \div 8$	**9.** $15 \div 3$	**10.** $24 \div 6$
11. $48 \div 8$	**12.** $24 \div 8$	**13.** $14 \div 7$	**14.** $35 \div 7$	**15.** $82 \div 1$
16. $63 \div 7$	**17.** $30 \div 5$	**18.** $31 \div 1$	**19.** $42 \div 7$	**20.** $32 \div 8$
21. $52 \div 4$	**22.** $96 \div 8$	**23.** $63 \div 3$	**24.** $90 \div 6$	**25.** $48 \div 6$
26. $36 \div 2$	**27.** $57 \div 3$	**28.** $14 \div 2$	**29.** $56 \div 8$	**30.** $97 \div 1$

Answer All the Questions Below:

1. $81 \div 3$	**2.** $24 \div 8$	**3.** $44 \div 1$	**4.** $15 \div 3$	**5.** $78 \div 6$
6. $45 \div 9$	**7.** $24 \div 6$	**8.** $16 \div 4$	**9.** $42 \div 7$	**10.** $36 \div 1$
11. $33 \div 3$	**12.** $38 \div 2$	**13.** $27 \div 9$	**14.** $45 \div 9$	**15.** $36 \div 9$
16. $40 \div 5$	**17.** $80 \div 8$	**18.** $64 \div 8$	**19.** $35 \div 7$	**20.** $80 \div 8$
21. $30 \div 5$	**22.** $11 \div 1$	**23.** $62 \div 1$	**24.** $30 \div 6$	**25.** $88 \div 8$
26. $16 \div 8$	**27.** $72 \div 6$	**28.** $36 \div 4$	**29.** $88 \div 8$	**30.** $81 \div 9$

Answer All the Questions Below:

1. $40 \div 8$	2. $42 \div 6$	3. $55 \div 5$	4. $35 \div 5$	5. $42 \div 6$
6. $92 \div 4$	7. $16 \div 1$	8. $83 \div 1$	9. $84 \div 6$	10. $16 \div 1$
11. $78 \div 6$	12. $42 \div 1$	13. $45 \div 9$	14. $68 \div 2$	15. $12 \div 6$
16. $84 \div 3$	17. $14 \div 2$	18. $90 \div 9$	19. $68 \div 4$	20. $72 \div 8$
21. $48 \div 8$	22. $28 \div 2$	23. $60 \div 5$	24. $86 \div 2$	25. $98 \div 7$
26. $44 \div 4$	27. $48 \div 4$	28. $63 \div 7$	29. $56 \div 4$	30. $44 \div 1$

DIVISION

2-Digit

1. $28 \div 7$	**2.** $90 \div 5$	**3.** $62 \div 1$	**4.** $84 \div 4$	**5.** $12 \div 1$
6. $42 \div 7$	**7.** $28 \div 4$	**8.** $36 \div 3$	**9.** $65 \div 5$	**10.** $90 \div 2$
11. $80 \div 5$	**12.** $65 \div 1$	**13.** $81 \div 9$	**14.** $80 \div 2$	**15.** $30 \div 3$
16. $27 \div 9$	**17.** $87 \div 3$	**18.** $49 \div 7$	**19.** $72 \div 6$	**20.** $80 \div 1$
21. $28 \div 7$	**22.** $36 \div 4$	**23.** $48 \div 4$	**24.** $21 \div 3$	**25.** $76 \div 1$
26. $22 \div 1$	**27.** $64 \div 8$	**28.** $54 \div 2$	**29.** $54 \div 2$	**30.** $21 \div 3$

Answer All the Questions Below:

1. $720 \div 80$	**2.** $690 \div 46$	**3.** $186 \div 62$	**4.** $814 \div 37$	**5.** $426 \div 71$
6. $840 \div 70$	**7.** $840 \div 60$	**8.** $140 \div 70$	**9.** $987 \div 47$	**10.** $624 \div 24$
11. $675 \div 25$	**12.** $819 \div 21$	**13.** $396 \div 18$	**14.** $882 \div 63$	**15.** $840 \div 5$
16. $172 \div 86$	**17.** $459 \div 27$	**18.** $730 \div 73$	**19.** $540 \div 54$	**20.** $686 \div 98$
21. $900 \div 15$	**22.** $969 \div 19$	**23.** $456 \div 57$	**24.** $760 \div 38$	**25.** $630 \div 70$
26. $374 \div 17$	**27.** $348 \div 58$	**28.** $440 \div 10$	**29.** $368 \div 92$	**30.** $488 \div 61$

1. 985 ÷ 5	**2.** 588 ÷ 98	**3.** 532 ÷ 19	**4.** 648 ÷ 81	**5.** 120 ÷ 60
6. 666 ÷ 74	**7.** 425 ÷ 85	**8.** 836 ÷ 19	**9.** 285 ÷ 95	**10.** 605 ÷ 55
11. 140 ÷ 5	**12.** 550 ÷ 50	**13.** 784 ÷ 98	**14.** 924 ÷ 77	**15.** 550 ÷ 11
16. 440 ÷ 40	**17.** 728 ÷ 56	**18.** 868 ÷ 4	**19.** 216 ÷ 8	**20.** 388 ÷ 97
21. 594 ÷ 66	**22.** 171 ÷ 57	**23.** 660 ÷ 66	**24.** 936 ÷ 72	**25.** 729 ÷ 81
26. 291 ÷ 97	**27.** 776 ÷ 8	**28.** 396 ÷ 36	**29.** 333 ÷ 9	**30.** 351 ÷ 13

Answer All the Questions Below:

1. 611 ÷ 47	2. 800 ÷ 80	3. 469 ÷ 67	4. 273 ÷ 39	5. 552 ÷ 92
6. 742 ÷ 53	7. 315 ÷ 45	8. 792 ÷ 99	9. 376 ÷ 94	10. 594 ÷ 27
11. 570 ÷ 57	12. 616 ÷ 77	13. 448 ÷ 14	14. 320 ÷ 64	15. 249 ÷ 83
16. 400 ÷ 1	17. 352 ÷ 16	18. 810 ÷ 54	19. 360 ÷ 60	20. 924 ÷ 42
21. 264 ÷ 88	22. 119 ÷ 17	23. 600 ÷ 15	24. 702 ÷ 27	25. 267 ÷ 3
26. 147 ÷ 49	27. 798 ÷ 57	28. 304 ÷ 76	29. 488 ÷ 4	30. 984 ÷ 41

1.
261
÷ 87

2.
680
÷ 85

3.
210
÷ 21

4.
544
÷ 32

5.
750
÷ 75

6.
429
÷ 13

7.
680
÷ 68

8.
732
÷ 12

9.
204
÷ 68

10.
672
÷ 84

11.
294
÷ 98

12.
160
÷ 20

13.
708
÷ 59

14.
915
÷ 61

15.
476
÷ 34

16.
776
÷ 97

17.
476
÷ 68

18.
477
÷ 53

19.
261
÷ 87

20.
294
÷ 6

21.
255
÷ 15

22.
406
÷ 58

23.
225
÷ 75

24.
452
÷ 1

25.
540
÷ 90

26.
790
÷ 79

27.
624
÷ 26

28.
620
÷ 31

29.
319
÷ 29

30.
352
÷ 88

DIVISION

3-Digit

Answer All the Questions Below:

1. $658 \div 7$	**2.** $990 \div 45$	**3.** $768 \div 96$	**4.** $462 \div 42$	**5.** $120 \div 15$
6. $986 \div 58$	**7.** $520 \div 20$	**8.** $748 \div 22$	**9.** $486 \div 54$	**10.** $696 \div 87$
11. $783 \div 87$	**12.** $560 \div 80$	**13.** $324 \div 9$	**14.** $882 \div 42$	**15.** $350 \div 50$
16. $697 \div 41$	**17.** $976 \div 16$	**18.** $840 \div 28$	**19.** $237 \div 79$	**20.** $768 \div 48$
21. $144 \div 24$	**22.** $920 \div 46$	**23.** $806 \div 62$	**24.** $880 \div 88$	**25.** $282 \div 6$
26. $828 \div 36$	**27.** $425 \div 85$	**28.** $518 \div 74$	**29.** $936 \div 78$	**30.** $810 \div 27$

Answer All the Questions Below:

1.
$4,108 \div 26$

2.
$6,944 \div 16$

3.
$6,384 \div 16$

4.
$5,376 \div 32$

5.
$5,766 \div 93$

6.
$7,268 \div 23$

7.
$6,348 \div 46$

8.
$9,504 \div 54$

9.
$9,541 \div 29$

10.
$3,150 \div 45$

11.
$6,956 \div 47$

12.
$9,135 \div 21$

13.
$8,624 \div 11$

14.
$7,124 \div 52$

15.
$3,050 \div 25$

16.
$6,708 \div 26$

17.
$1,725 \div 23$

18.
$2,714 \div 46$

19.
$8,730 \div 15$

20.
$3,519 \div 69$

21.
$3,575 \div 65$

22.
$7,260 \div 44$

23.
$5,075 \div 25$

24.
$1,856 \div 64$

Answer All the Questions Below:

1. 5,402 ÷ 37	**2.** 5,448 ÷ 24	**3.** 7,423 ÷ 13	**4.** 9,500 ÷ 95
5. 8,610 ÷ 70	**6.** 5,928 ÷ 78	**7.** 8,432 ÷ 17	**8.** 7,242 ÷ 71
9. 4,209 ÷ 61	**10.** 9,516 ÷ 78	**11.** 4,968 ÷ 69	**12.** 5,032 ÷ 74
13. 4,420 ÷ 65	**14.** 4,588 ÷ 31	**15.** 2,850 ÷ 38	**16.** 8,395 ÷ 73
17. 9,823 ÷ 47	**18.** 4,316 ÷ 83	**19.** 3,045 ÷ 87	**20.** 7,868 ÷ 14
21. 7,938 ÷ 54	**22.** 6,279 ÷ 69	**23.** 8,170 ÷ 95	**24.** 9,193 ÷ 29

DIVISION

4-Digit

1. $2{,}640 \div 40$	**2.** $7{,}776 \div 96$	**3.** $2{,}480 \div 62$	**4.** $6{,}720 \div 80$
5. $6{,}405 \div 61$	**6.** $8{,}395 \div 73$	**7.** $9{,}212 \div 98$	**8.** $7{,}640 \div 10$
9. $2{,}698 \div 71$	**10.** $5{,}632 \div 64$	**11.** $7{,}028 \div 14$	**12.** $5{,}810 \div 83$
13. $5{,}986 \div 82$	**14.** $5{,}735 \div 31$	**15.** $6{,}900 \div 23$	**16.** $4{,}095 \div 65$
17. $2{,}790 \div 45$	**18.** $4{,}074 \div 14$	**19.** $8{,}050 \div 70$	**20.** $5{,}684 \div 98$
21. $2{,}240 \div 20$	**22.** $8{,}342 \div 97$	**23.** $4{,}089 \div 87$	**24.** $3{,}276 \div 18$

DIVISION

1.	2.	3.	4.
$2{,}255 \div 55$	$1{,}872 \div 39$	$7{,}200 \div 48$	$8{,}960 \div 70$

5.	6.	7.	8.
$2{,}835 \div 63$	$8{,}178 \div 58$	$4{,}374 \div 81$	$9{,}555 \div 39$

9.	10.	11.	12.
$6{,}804 \div 28$	$7{,}275 \div 97$	$6{,}444 \div 12$	$6{,}665 \div 31$

13.	14.	15.	16.
$6{,}580 \div 28$	$4{,}180 \div 55$	$2{,}175 \div 29$	$9{,}636 \div 66$

17.	18.	19.	20.
$9{,}540 \div 36$	$5{,}115 \div 55$	$8{,}246 \div 38$	$2{,}783 \div 23$

21.	22.	23.	24.
$8{,}316 \div 28$	$8{,}372 \div 91$	$7{,}860 \div 10$	$8{,}280 \div 69$

Answer All the Questions Below:

1.
   2,385
÷   53

2.
   7,720
÷   40

3.
   3,900
÷   75

4.
   8,547
÷   77

5.
   1,936
÷   88

6.
   8,908
÷   68

7.
   4,664
÷   88

8.
   6,776
÷   28

9.
   7,150
÷   65

10.
   9,460
÷   86

11.
   5,640
÷   94

12.
   5,922
÷   94

13.
   1,817
÷   79

14.
   7,990
÷   34

15.
   8,740
÷   76

16.
   7,068
÷   38

17.
   8,640
÷   36

18.
   5,985
÷   21

19.
   9,486
÷   93

20.
   3,441
÷   37

21.
   2,550
÷   17

22.
   5,871
÷   57

23.
   9,792
÷   68

24.
   5,304
÷   52

DIVISION

4-Digit

Answer All the Questions Below:

1.
$$7{,}387 \div 83$$

2.
$$9{,}440 \div 20$$

3.
$$5{,}833 \div 19$$

4.
$$5{,}727 \div 69$$

5.
$$6{,}594 \div 21$$

6.
$$9{,}600 \div 80$$

7.
$$3{,}120 \div 60$$

8.
$$6{,}105 \div 55$$

9.
$$9{,}225 \div 25$$

10.
$$1{,}344 \div 28$$

11.
$$7{,}956 \div 68$$

12.
$$2{,}496 \div 48$$

13.
$$5{,}018 \div 13$$

14.
$$6{,}468 \div 66$$

15.
$$8{,}175 \div 25$$

16.
$$8{,}721 \div 27$$

17.
$$9{,}120 \div 96$$

18.
$$7{,}524 \div 76$$

19.
$$7{,}968 \div 96$$

20.
$$1{,}368 \div 76$$

21.
$$9{,}266 \div 82$$

22.
$$3{,}050 \div 61$$

23.
$$2{,}226 \div 53$$

24.
$$9{,}100 \div 50$$

Answers
1-4

Set 1

1.	2.	3.	4.	5.
5 + 9 —— 14	4 + 4 —— 8	2 + 7 —— 9	3 + 5 —— 8	1 + 3 —— 4
6.	**7.**	**8.**	**9.**	**10.**
6 + 3 —— 9	6 + 9 —— 15	9 + 9 —— 18	9 + 4 —— 13	6 + 3 —— 9
11.	**12.**	**13.**	**14.**	**15.**
5 + 0 —— 5	5 + 3 —— 8	2 + 6 —— 8	7 + 3 —— 10	2 + 3 —— 5
16.	**17.**	**18.**	**19.**	**20.**
8 + 8 —— 16	8 + 6 —— 14	2 + 3 —— 5	2 + 8 —— 10	1 + 2 —— 3

Set 2

1.	2.	3.	4.	5.
9 + 8 —— 17	7 + 6 —— 13	7 + 4 —— 11	1 + 6 —— 7	3 + 8 —— 11
6.	**7.**	**8.**	**9.**	**10.**
3 + 5 —— 8	1 + 4 —— 5	4 + 2 —— 6	6 + 5 —— 11	6 + 0 —— 6
11.	**12.**	**13.**	**14.**	**15.**
6 + 2 —— 8	0 + 1 —— 1	5 + 8 —— 13	1 + 8 —— 9	7 + 2 —— 9
16.	**17.**	**18.**	**19.**	**20.**
4 + 1 —— 5	0 + 8 —— 8	3 + 0 —— 3	6 + 0 —— 6	2 + 9 —— 11

Set 3

1.	2.	3.	4.	5.
4 + 2 —— 6	6 + 3 —— 9	3 + 4 —— 7	3 + 9 —— 12	6 + 1 —— 7
6.	**7.**	**8.**	**9.**	**10.**
0 + 0 —— 0	4 + 8 —— 12	5 + 3 —— 8	5 + 0 —— 5	9 + 7 —— 16
11.	**12.**	**13.**	**14.**	**15.**
0 + 2 —— 2	9 + 7 —— 16	7 + 2 —— 9	0 + 1 —— 1	5 + 9 —— 14
16.	**17.**	**18.**	**19.**	**20.**
7 + 9 —— 16	9 + 3 —— 12	6 + 1 —— 7	0 + 5 —— 5	1 + 9 —— 10

Set 4

1.	2.	3.	4.	5.
0 + 4 —— 4	5 + 1 —— 6	3 + 8 —— 11	3 + 9 —— 12	6 + 6 —— 12
6.	**7.**	**8.**	**9.**	**10.**
9 + 7 —— 16	5 + 2 —— 7	8 + 9 —— 17	0 + 8 —— 8	7 + 0 —— 7
11.	**12.**	**13.**	**14.**	**15.**
9 + 1 —— 10	6 + 9 —— 15	7 + 9 —— 16	1 + 5 —— 6	9 + 7 —— 16
16.	**17.**	**18.**	**19.**	**20.**
0 + 6 —— 6	4 + 7 —— 11	5 + 7 —— 12	5 + 6 —— 11	6 + 0 —— 6

Answers
5-8

Set 1

#	Problem	Answer
1.	46 + 77	123
2.	95 + 23	118
3.	28 + 59	87
4.	46 + 85	131
5.	87 + 58	145
6.	67 + 43	110
7.	94 + 86	180
8.	47 + 92	139
9.	38 + 53	91
10.	96 + 95	191
11.	24 + 72	96
12.	87 + 14	101
13.	23 + 85	108
14.	63 + 34	97
15.	55 + 43	98
16.	80 + 89	169
17.	91 + 18	109
18.	89 + 71	160
19.	12 + 44	56
20.	26 + 28	54
21.	19 + 76	95
22.	63 + 73	136
23.	65 + 65	130
24.	65 + 69	134
25.	57 + 28	85
26.	18 + 40	58
27.	10 + 57	67
28.	57 + 60	117
29.	21 + 31	52
30.	67 + 40	107

Set 2

#	Problem	Answer
1.	92 + 53	145
2.	73 + 52	125
3.	77 + 11	88
4.	77 + 51	128
5.	90 + 10	100
6.	59 + 98	157
7.	17 + 57	74
8.	90 + 23	113
9.	21 + 68	89
10.	32 + 31	63
11.	62 + 81	143
12.	27 + 35	62
13.	52 + 60	112
14.	39 + 88	127
15.	18 + 68	86
16.	59 + 60	119
17.	18 + 65	83
18.	29 + 89	118
19.	92 + 73	165
20.	53 + 86	139
21.	39 + 35	74
22.	69 + 43	112
23.	86 + 86	172
24.	89 + 27	116
25.	46 + 12	58
26.	79 + 37	116
27.	48 + 58	106
28.	31 + 93	124
29.	12 + 82	94
30.	48 + 33	81

Set 3

#	Problem	Answer
1.	27 + 78	105
2.	51 + 79	130
3.	87 + 44	131
4.	83 + 94	177
5.	11 + 88	99
6.	85 + 51	136
7.	67 + 80	147
8.	65 + 40	105
9.	13 + 80	93
10.	15 + 16	31
11.	58 + 42	100
12.	38 + 93	131
13.	23 + 83	106
14.	15 + 86	101
15.	64 + 38	102
16.	28 + 55	83
17.	82 + 55	137
18.	93 + 76	169
19.	73 + 52	125
20.	35 + 69	104
21.	80 + 24	104
22.	14 + 64	78
23.	85 + 29	114
24.	27 + 87	114
25.	79 + 49	128
26.	41 + 71	112
27.	45 + 75	120
28.	13 + 25	38
29.	85 + 27	112
30.	43 + 89	132

Set 4

#	Problem	Answer
1.	84 + 77	161
2.	83 + 27	110
3.	32 + 25	57
4.	43 + 47	90
5.	50 + 40	90
6.	51 + 99	150
7.	28 + 36	64
8.	39 + 30	69
9.	52 + 67	119
10.	10 + 39	49
11.	98 + 29	127
12.	81 + 45	126
13.	46 + 81	127
14.	28 + 23	51
15.	94 + 73	167
16.	54 + 30	84
17.	71 + 73	144
18.	28 + 40	68
19.	90 + 53	143
20.	63 + 14	77
21.	44 + 27	71
22.	45 + 49	94
23.	67 + 86	153
24.	15 + 19	34
25.	51 + 98	149
26.	66 + 80	146
27.	55 + 26	81
28.	61 + 53	114
29.	12 + 72	84
30.	15 + 11	26

Answers
9-12

<table>
<tr><td>1.
47
+ 61
108</td><td>2.
67
+ 96
163</td><td>3.
28
+ 84
112</td><td>4.
29
+ 37
66</td><td>5.
63
+ 75
138</td></tr>
<tr><td>6.
32
+ 45
77</td><td>7.
96
+ 91
187</td><td>8.
23
+ 59
82</td><td>9.
60
+ 83
143</td><td>10.
29
+ 47
76</td></tr>
<tr><td>11.
11
+ 36
47</td><td>12.
34
+ 82
116</td><td>13.
47
+ 86
133</td><td>14.
89
+ 45
134</td><td>15.
92
+ 94
186</td></tr>
<tr><td>16.
33
+ 45
78</td><td>17.
13
+ 45
58</td><td>18.
33
+ 88
121</td><td>19.
61
+ 19
80</td><td>20.
53
+ 26
79</td></tr>
<tr><td>21.
83
+ 31
114</td><td>22.
60
+ 33
93</td><td>23.
41
+ 82
123</td><td>24.
16
+ 22
38</td><td>25.
47
+ 13
60</td></tr>
<tr><td>26.
90
+ 47
137</td><td>27.
16
+ 74
90</td><td>28.
24
+ 56
80</td><td>29.
68
+ 70
138</td><td>30.
42
+ 12
54</td></tr>
</table>

<table>
<tr><td>1.
515
+ 726
1,241</td><td>2.
509
+ 610
1,119</td><td>3.
567
+ 608
1,175</td><td>4.
672
+ 362
1,034</td><td>5.
711
+ 743
1,454</td></tr>
<tr><td>6.
246
+ 287
533</td><td>7.
476
+ 665
1,141</td><td>8.
570
+ 824
1,394</td><td>9.
584
+ 985
1,569</td><td>10.
699
+ 373
1,072</td></tr>
<tr><td>11.
885
+ 134
1,019</td><td>12.
265
+ 855
1,120</td><td>13.
865
+ 633
1,498</td><td>14.
698
+ 202
900</td><td>15.
126
+ 353
479</td></tr>
<tr><td>16.
697
+ 143
840</td><td>17.
455
+ 792
1,247</td><td>18.
823
+ 214
1,037</td><td>19.
498
+ 969
1,467</td><td>20.
539
+ 578
1,117</td></tr>
<tr><td>21.
540
+ 146
686</td><td>22.
944
+ 484
1,428</td><td>23.
494
+ 749
1,243</td><td>24.
247
+ 338
585</td><td>25.
128
+ 783
911</td></tr>
<tr><td>26.
152
+ 996
1,148</td><td>27.
727
+ 896
1,623</td><td>28.
143
+ 302
445</td><td>29.
229
+ 793
1,022</td><td>30.
261
+ 705
966</td></tr>
</table>

<table>
<tr><td>1.
693
+ 333
1,026</td><td>2.
466
+ 971
1,437</td><td>3.
447
+ 375
822</td><td>4.
176
+ 865
1,041</td><td>5.
904
+ 599
1,503</td></tr>
<tr><td>6.
222
+ 465
687</td><td>7.
690
+ 706
1,396</td><td>8.
618
+ 800
1,418</td><td>9.
656
+ 791
1,447</td><td>10.
382
+ 692
1,074</td></tr>
<tr><td>11.
411
+ 621
1,032</td><td>12.
536
+ 254
790</td><td>13.
581
+ 690
1,271</td><td>14.
402
+ 685
1,087</td><td>15.
617
+ 525
1,142</td></tr>
<tr><td>16.
918
+ 245
1,163</td><td>17.
712
+ 211
923</td><td>18.
497
+ 322
819</td><td>19.
630
+ 582
1,212</td><td>20.
919
+ 423
1,342</td></tr>
<tr><td>21.
387
+ 424
811</td><td>22.
345
+ 550
895</td><td>23.
229
+ 729
958</td><td>24.
891
+ 919
1,810</td><td>25.
896
+ 648
1,544</td></tr>
<tr><td>26.
680
+ 111
791</td><td>27.
163
+ 412
575</td><td>28.
224
+ 906
1,130</td><td>29.
615
+ 446
1,061</td><td>30.
548
+ 677
1,225</td></tr>
</table>

<table>
<tr><td>1.
707
+ 683
1,390</td><td>2.
532
+ 733
1,265</td><td>3.
543
+ 755
1,298</td><td>4.
299
+ 455
754</td><td>5.
135
+ 944
1,079</td></tr>
<tr><td>6.
409
+ 423
832</td><td>7.
443
+ 737
1,180</td><td>8.
688
+ 655
1,343</td><td>9.
771
+ 369
1,140</td><td>10.
774
+ 658
1,432</td></tr>
<tr><td>11.
776
+ 934
1,710</td><td>12.
324
+ 128
452</td><td>13.
284
+ 799
1,083</td><td>14.
988
+ 640
1,628</td><td>15.
284
+ 310
594</td></tr>
<tr><td>16.
279
+ 278
557</td><td>17.
890
+ 428
1,318</td><td>18.
499
+ 742
1,241</td><td>19.
975
+ 180
1,155</td><td>20.
209
+ 379
588</td></tr>
<tr><td>21.
701
+ 556
1,257</td><td>22.
267
+ 798
1,065</td><td>23.
141
+ 582
723</td><td>24.
555
+ 789
1,344</td><td>25.
417
+ 248
665</td></tr>
<tr><td>26.
622
+ 847
1,469</td><td>27.
294
+ 761
1,055</td><td>28.
969
+ 732
1,701</td><td>29.
862
+ 293
1,155</td><td>30.
337
+ 179
516</td></tr>
</table>

Answers
13-16

Box 1

1. 915 + 929 = 1,844	2. 542 + 299 = 841	3. 534 + 312 = 846	4. 757 + 180 = 937	5. 539 + 556 = 1,095
6. 502 + 155 = 657	7. 745 + 867 = 1,612	8. 912 + 182 = 1,094	9. 478 + 646 = 1,124	10. 671 + 852 = 1,523
11. 550 + 668 = 1,218	12. 512 + 473 = 985	13. 203 + 838 = 1,041	14. 574 + 195 = 769	15. 912 + 605 = 1,517
16. 590 + 332 = 922	17. 767 + 782 = 1,549	18. 394 + 125 = 519	19. 999 + 409 = 1,408	20. 422 + 505 = 927
21. 919 + 509 = 1,428	22. 617 + 201 = 818	23. 965 + 871 = 1,836	24. 803 + 176 = 979	25. 725 + 568 = 1,293
26. 975 + 120 = 1,095	27. 821 + 545 = 1,366	28. 984 + 512 = 1,496	29. 811 + 739 = 1,550	30. 147 + 814 = 961

Box 2

1. 674 + 278 = 952	2. 114 + 969 = 1,083	3. 838 + 479 = 1,317	4. 662 + 144 = 806	5. 128 + 619 = 747
6. 875 + 189 = 1,064	7. 576 + 373 = 949	8. 814 + 553 = 1,367	9. 403 + 531 = 934	10. 750 + 369 = 1,119
11. 352 + 826 = 1,178	12. 668 + 802 = 1,470	13. 776 + 549 = 1,325	14. 755 + 850 = 1,605	15. 545 + 554 = 1,099
16. 192 + 523 = 715	17. 477 + 541 = 1,018	18. 380 + 456 = 836	19. 712 + 303 = 1,015	20. 126 + 180 = 306
21. 188 + 464 = 652	22. 532 + 923 = 1,455	23. 394 + 202 = 596	24. 417 + 694 = 1,111	25. 300 + 702 = 1,002
26. 692 + 266 = 958	27. 760 + 160 = 920	28. 958 + 965 = 1,923	29. 692 + 852 = 1,544	30. 757 + 354 = 1,111

Box 3

1. 5,825 + 8,121 = 13,946	2. 5,077 + 8,582 = 13,659	3. 2,464 + 4,571 = 7,035	4. 3,775 + 8,477 = 12,252
5. 5,178 + 9,745 = 14,923	6. 4,402 + 3,768 = 8,170	7. 5,506 + 8,046 = 13,552	8. 5,758 + 2,867 = 8,625
9. 7,764 + 4,661 = 12,425	10. 9,565 + 7,698 = 17,263	11. 8,677 + 8,042 = 16,719	12. 2,247 + 5,583 = 7,830
13. 7,927 + 3,631 = 11,558	14. 8,041 + 4,459 = 12,500	15. 5,477 + 9,249 = 14,726	16. 4,241 + 8,131 = 12,372
17. 5,138 + 2,311 = 7,449	18. 4,804 + 1,989 = 6,793	19. 8,215 + 6,879 = 15,094	20. 8,165 + 6,512 = 14,677
21. 4,167 + 7,399 = 11,566	22. 4,426 + 6,478 = 10,904	23. 3,134 + 1,833 = 4,967	24. 2,662 + 5,461 = 8,123

Box 4

1. 2,165 + 2,617 = 4,782	2. 7,662 + 3,876 = 11,538	3. 8,201 + 4,401 = 12,602	4. 8,373 + 2,738 = 11,111
5. 6,430 + 2,220 = 8,650	6. 2,776 + 7,125 = 9,901	7. 6,751 + 3,571 = 10,322	8. 6,103 + 4,322 = 10,425
9. 9,715 + 3,056 = 12,771	10. 2,577 + 8,355 = 10,932	11. 5,031 + 7,029 = 12,060	12. 9,090 + 5,319 = 14,409
13. 5,876 + 2,772 = 8,648	14. 4,530 + 5,512 = 10,042	15. 5,706 + 5,056 = 10,762	16. 2,855 + 6,083 = 8,938
17. 4,733 + 4,391 = 9,124	18. 3,816 + 7,357 = 11,173	19. 6,635 + 1,736 = 8,371	20. 3,823 + 2,033 = 5,856
21. 1,904 + 5,238 = 7,142	22. 6,111 + 3,348 = 9,459	23. 6,811 + 8,283 = 15,094	24. 5,824 + 5,256 = 11,080

Answers
17-20

Box 1

1. 3,678 + 9,338 = 13,016	**2.** 7,175 + 6,768 = 13,943	**3.** 6,628 + 8,454 = 15,082	**4.** 5,776 + 5,791 = 11,567
5. 9,049 + 1,944 = 10,993	**6.** 6,531 + 5,080 = 11,611	**7.** 3,610 + 4,410 = 8,020	**8.** 8,288 + 2,026 = 10,314
9. 2,254 + 8,864 = 11,118	**10.** 8,131 + 8,732 = 16,863	**11.** 9,369 + 6,461 = 15,830	**12.** 8,051 + 1,601 = 9,652
13. 4,619 + 3,258 = 7,877	**14.** 7,189 + 1,832 = 9,021	**15.** 2,524 + 8,931 = 11,455	**16.** 8,830 + 9,788 = 18,618
17. 1,746 + 9,839 = 11,585	**18.** 6,537 + 6,168 = 12,705	**19.** 5,568 + 1,686 = 7,254	**20.** 1,732 + 2,681 = 4,413
21. 8,414 + 2,823 = 11,237	**22.** 7,666 + 6,070 = 13,736	**23.** 4,843 + 1,932 = 6,775	**24.** 7,388 + 5,731 = 13,119

Box 2

1. 5,126 + 9,732 = 14,858	**2.** 9,636 + 2,597 = 12,233	**3.** 4,350 + 7,164 = 11,514	**4.** 3,461 + 4,148 = 7,609
5. 6,030 + 5,310 = 11,340	**6.** 5,638 + 6,359 = 11,997	**7.** 8,896 + 2,798 = 11,694	**8.** 7,183 + 2,032 = 9,215
9. 4,267 + 5,460 = 9,727	**10.** 6,560 + 5,707 = 12,267	**11.** 9,220 + 4,149 = 13,369	**12.** 7,710 + 7,315 = 15,025
13. 8,519 + 6,187 = 14,706	**14.** 6,441 + 7,486 = 13,927	**15.** 3,949 + 6,574 = 10,523	**16.** 6,751 + 9,016 = 15,767
17. 9,615 + 3,445 = 13,060	**18.** 4,357 + 8,996 = 13,353	**19.** 7,107 + 5,020 = 12,127	**20.** 3,680 + 9,902 = 13,582
21. 2,466 + 4,846 = 7,312	**22.** 7,248 + 4,861 = 12,109	**23.** 8,704 + 5,537 = 14,241	**24.** 9,092 + 8,045 = 17,137

Box 3

1. 5,975 + 8,912 = 14,887	**2.** 2,488 + 3,096 = 5,584	**3.** 5,273 + 9,797 = 15,070	**4.** 2,274 + 8,368 = 10,642
5. 2,067 + 6,598 = 8,665	**6.** 2,777 + 5,155 = 7,932	**7.** 6,227 + 7,250 = 13,477	**8.** 1,978 + 4,238 = 6,216
9. 1,896 + 4,430 = 6,326	**10.** 5,340 + 7,373 = 12,713	**11.** 6,707 + 3,138 = 9,845	**12.** 6,851 + 5,124 = 11,975
13. 8,083 + 3,879 = 11,962	**14.** 7,666 + 4,193 = 11,859	**15.** 3,626 + 3,647 = 7,273	**16.** 9,550 + 6,927 = 16,477
17. 3,684 + 4,321 = 8,005	**18.** 6,657 + 2,278 = 8,935	**19.** 5,984 + 7,849 = 13,833	**20.** 2,986 + 6,403 = 9,389
21. 7,827 + 3,988 = 11,815	**22.** 2,991 + 9,086 = 12,077	**23.** 9,742 + 5,682 = 15,424	**24.** 6,638 + 4,096 = 10,734

Box 4

1. 9 − 6 = 3	**2.** 6 − 3 = 3	**3.** 9 − 2 = 7	**4.** 9 − 2 = 7	**5.** 8 − 2 = 6
6. 6 − 5 = 1	**7.** 2 − 2 = 0	**8.** 8 − 3 = 5	**9.** 2 − 1 = 1	**10.** 6 − 5 = 1
11. 1 − 1 = 0	**12.** 2 − 1 = 1	**13.** 9 − 7 = 2	**14.** 6 − 0 = 6	**15.** 2 − 0 = 2
16. 8 − 8 = 0	**17.** 2 − 1 = 1	**18.** 9 − 8 = 1	**19.** 7 − 1 = 6	**20.** 3 − 0 = 3

Answers
21-24

Box 1

1. 4 − 4 = 0	2. 7 − 7 = 0	3. 4 − 1 = 3	4. 9 − 8 = 1	5. 7 − 6 = 1
6. 9 − 4 = 5	7. 5 − 1 = 4	8. 7 − 6 = 1	9. 5 − 4 = 1	10. 8 − 1 = 7
11. 7 − 4 = 3	12. 5 − 0 = 5	13. 9 − 7 = 2	14. 3 − 3 = 0	15. 7 − 1 = 6
16. 7 − 6 = 1	17. 5 − 2 = 3	18. 8 − 8 = 0	19. 9 − 0 = 9	20. 8 − 3 = 5

Box 2

1. 4 − 1 = 3	2. 7 − 2 = 5	3. 5 − 1 = 4	4. 6 − 4 = 2	5. 9 − 0 = 9
6. 3 − 1 = 2	7. 5 − 2 = 3	8. 8 − 1 = 7	9. 6 − 4 = 2	10. 9 − 6 = 3
11. 6 − 6 = 0	12. 6 − 3 = 3	13. 8 − 1 = 7	14. 2 − 0 = 2	15. 4 − 4 = 0
16. 9 − 6 = 3	17. 8 − 7 = 1	18. 6 − 2 = 4	19. 4 − 1 = 3	20. 4 − 2 = 2

Box 3

1. 9 − 2 = 7	2. 9 − 1 = 8	3. 7 − 7 = 0	4. 4 − 2 = 2	5. 2 − 1 = 1
6. 7 − 2 = 5	7. 9 − 3 = 6	8. 1 − 1 = 0	9. 9 − 4 = 5	10. 6 − 5 = 1
11. 4 − 1 = 3	12. 4 − 4 = 0	13. 5 − 1 = 4	14. 8 − 7 = 1	15. 5 − 2 = 3
16. 9 − 3 = 6	17. 5 − 2 = 3	18. 4 − 2 = 2	19. 6 − 1 = 5	20. 9 − 4 = 5

Box 4

1. 87 − 27 = 60	2. 86 − 67 = 19	3. 94 − 66 = 28	4. 61 − 43 = 18	5. 89 − 68 = 21
6. 94 − 59 = 35	7. 79 − 71 = 8	8. 56 − 44 = 12	9. 60 − 46 = 14	10. 82 − 34 = 48
11. 49 − 11 = 38	12. 41 − 30 = 11	13. 78 − 73 = 5	14. 63 − 40 = 23	15. 99 − 71 = 28
16. 78 − 22 = 56	17. 91 − 74 = 17	18. 98 − 48 = 50	19. 84 − 51 = 33	20. 73 − 52 = 21
21. 49 − 13 = 36	22. 64 − 64 = 0	23. 58 − 36 = 22	24. 59 − 50 = 9	25. 58 − 57 = 1
26. 46 − 31 = 15	27. 96 − 61 = 35	28. 79 − 28 = 51	29. 66 − 30 = 36	30. 95 − 44 = 51

Answers
25-28

Set 25

1. 76 − 12 = 64	2. 19 − 15 = 4	3. 73 − 46 = 27	4. 95 − 41 = 54	5. 90 − 21 = 69
6. 72 − 17 = 55	7. 44 − 42 = 2	8. 43 − 20 = 23	9. 89 − 41 = 48	10. 80 − 22 = 58
11. 68 − 52 = 16	12. 78 − 69 = 9	13. 61 − 34 = 27	14. 97 − 54 = 43	15. 45 − 41 = 4
16. 55 − 29 = 26	17. 92 − 34 = 58	18. 82 − 68 = 14	19. 62 − 26 = 36	20. 60 − 30 = 30
21. 78 − 63 = 15	22. 80 − 34 = 46	23. 87 − 28 = 59	24. 35 − 28 = 7	25. 83 − 65 = 18
26. 74 − 36 = 38	27. 97 − 60 = 37	28. 80 − 14 = 66	29. 89 − 42 = 47	30. 81 − 16 = 65

Set 26

1. 72 − 53 = 19	2. 53 − 43 = 10	3. 91 − 73 = 18	4. 25 − 12 = 13	5. 43 − 28 = 15
6. 70 − 43 = 27	7. 69 − 22 = 47	8. 31 − 23 = 8	9. 66 − 25 = 41	10. 81 − 53 = 28
11. 92 − 63 = 29	12. 84 − 29 = 55	13. 58 − 49 = 9	14. 67 − 18 = 49	15. 66 − 53 = 13
16. 35 − 17 = 18	17. 77 − 59 = 18	18. 97 − 90 = 7	19. 51 − 35 = 16	20. 22 − 11 = 11
21. 86 − 54 = 32	22. 58 − 22 = 36	23. 84 − 19 = 65	24. 84 − 28 = 56	25. 98 − 96 = 2
26. 79 − 52 = 27	27. 66 − 13 = 53	28. 31 − 16 = 15	29. 91 − 75 = 16	30. 63 − 10 = 53

Set 27

1. 63 − 21 = 42	2. 74 − 68 = 6	3. 32 − 28 = 4	4. 96 − 92 = 4	5. 66 − 14 = 52
6. 70 − 33 = 37	7. 84 − 69 = 15	8. 68 − 19 = 49	9. 34 − 31 = 3	10. 80 − 76 = 4
11. 84 − 66 = 18	12. 81 − 56 = 25	13. 43 − 31 = 12	14. 77 − 20 = 57	15. 84 − 15 = 69
16. 38 − 15 = 23	17. 67 − 33 = 34	18. 57 − 14 = 43	19. 72 − 56 = 16	20. 74 − 52 = 22
21. 56 − 33 = 23	22. 95 − 79 = 16	23. 48 − 34 = 14	24. 69 − 37 = 32	25. 90 − 22 = 68
26. 66 − 51 = 15	27. 92 − 76 = 16	28. 75 − 29 = 46	29. 46 − 45 = 1	30. 56 − 36 = 20

Set 28

1. 71 − 68 = 3	2. 98 − 42 = 56	3. 89 − 77 = 12	4. 89 − 88 = 1	5. 67 − 37 = 30
6. 66 − 30 = 36	7. 86 − 32 = 54	8. 57 − 46 = 11	9. 77 − 39 = 38	10. 79 − 69 = 10
11. 41 − 30 = 11	12. 81 − 48 = 33	13. 91 − 61 = 30	14. 63 − 17 = 46	15. 83 − 46 = 37
16. 66 − 12 = 54	17. 70 − 51 = 19	18. 55 − 37 = 18	19. 98 − 78 = 20	20. 35 − 19 = 16
21. 63 − 29 = 34	22. 83 − 46 = 37	23. 77 − 38 = 39	24. 51 − 41 = 10	25. 90 − 24 = 66
26. 56 − 50 = 6	27. 34 − 25 = 9	28. 92 − 38 = 54	29. 72 − 28 = 44	30. 92 − 75 = 17

Answers
29-32

29

1. 216 − 188 = 28	2. 445 − 142 = 303	3. 676 − 615 = 61	4. 690 − 460 = 230	5. 729 − 420 = 309
6. 868 − 132 = 736	7. 470 − 241 = 229	8. 975 − 118 = 857	9. 298 − 161 = 137	10. 925 − 245 = 680
11. 750 − 619 = 131	12. 735 − 207 = 528	13. 529 − 505 = 24	14. 698 − 656 = 42	15. 299 − 226 = 73
16. 892 − 397 = 495	17. 917 − 882 = 35	18. 314 − 252 = 62	19. 972 − 310 = 662	20. 665 − 196 = 469
21. 993 − 832 = 161	22. 906 − 445 = 461	23. 726 − 619 = 107	24. 864 − 782 = 82	25. 568 − 446 = 122
26. 618 − 394 = 224	27. 617 − 450 = 167	28. 967 − 883 = 84	29. 588 − 495 = 93	30. 602 − 329 = 273

30

1. 683 − 111 = 572	2. 905 − 324 = 581	3. 226 − 176 = 50	4. 724 − 343 = 381	5. 440 − 409 = 31
6. 364 − 195 = 169	7. 906 − 744 = 162	8. 987 − 378 = 609	9. 288 − 122 = 166	10. 932 − 629 = 303
11. 926 − 317 = 609	12. 212 − 119 = 93	13. 241 − 229 = 12	14. 709 − 165 = 544	15. 571 − 173 = 398
16. 707 − 111 = 596	17. 377 − 311 = 66	18. 401 − 328 = 73	19. 576 − 329 = 247	20. 701 − 274 = 427
21. 812 − 201 = 611	22. 798 − 628 = 170	23. 484 − 252 = 232	24. 676 − 143 = 533	25. 744 − 324 = 420
26. 855 − 586 = 269	27. 968 − 282 = 686	28. 705 − 304 = 401	29. 620 − 331 = 289	30. 415 − 117 = 298

31

1. 665 − 522 = 143	2. 791 − 175 = 616	3. 950 − 943 = 7	4. 785 − 492 = 293	5. 582 − 128 = 454
6. 860 − 527 = 333	7. 936 − 223 = 713	8. 936 − 267 = 669	9. 945 − 623 = 322	10. 433 − 384 = 49
11. 781 − 567 = 214	12. 913 − 496 = 417	13. 337 − 199 = 138	14. 553 − 489 = 64	15. 342 − 279 = 63
16. 834 − 780 = 54	17. 969 − 403 = 566	18. 893 − 675 = 218	19. 706 − 621 = 85	20. 521 − 163 = 358
21. 837 − 391 = 446	22. 774 − 210 = 564	23. 768 − 603 = 165	24. 676 − 646 = 30	25. 614 − 508 = 106
26. 653 − 360 = 293	27. 773 − 264 = 509	28. 667 − 505 = 162	29. 423 − 198 = 225	30. 670 − 439 = 231

32

1. 944 − 815 = 129	2. 676 − 450 = 226	3. 968 − 280 = 688	4. 724 − 148 = 576	5. 423 − 355 = 68
6. 323 − 293 = 30	7. 898 − 593 = 305	8. 553 − 523 = 30	9. 409 − 135 = 274	10. 957 − 170 = 787
11. 816 − 410 = 406	12. 189 − 125 = 64	13. 577 − 134 = 443	14. 993 − 166 = 827	15. 854 − 450 = 404
16. 510 − 223 = 287	17. 574 − 532 = 42	18. 509 − 327 = 182	19. 558 − 184 = 374	20. 674 − 578 = 96
21. 793 − 355 = 438	22. 961 − 930 = 31	23. 979 − 334 = 645	24. 777 − 352 = 425	25. 982 − 609 = 373
26. 746 − 540 = 206	27. 315 − 277 = 38	28. 130 − 111 = 19	29. 918 − 527 = 391	30. 885 − 839 = 46

Answers
33-36

Page 33

1. 404 − 234 = 170	2. 389 − 307 = 82	3. 828 − 695 = 133	4. 924 − 539 = 385	5. 580 − 158 = 422
6. 606 − 355 = 251	7. 782 − 775 = 7	8. 992 − 319 = 673	9. 793 − 518 = 275	10. 609 − 437 = 172
11. 265 − 191 = 74	12. 926 − 339 = 587	13. 764 − 372 = 392	14. 629 − 412 = 217	15. 589 − 582 = 7
16. 475 − 270 = 205	17. 289 − 216 = 73	18. 396 − 188 = 208	19. 940 − 737 = 203	20. 981 − 889 = 92
21. 845 − 261 = 584	22. 661 − 602 = 59	23. 930 − 234 = 696	24. 795 − 347 = 448	25. 921 − 659 = 262
26. 646 − 455 = 191	27. 850 − 354 = 496	28. 535 − 138 = 397	29. 431 − 183 = 248	30. 490 − 421 = 69

Page 34

1. 9,941 − 6,578 = 3,363	2. 6,787 − 5,349 = 1,438	3. 9,940 − 5,593 = 4,347	4. 9,590 − 4,049 = 5,541
5. 5,078 − 3,430 = 1,648	6. 3,474 − 3,073 = 401	7. 9,881 − 9,336 = 545	8. 7,659 − 5,253 = 2,406
9. 9,541 − 5,171 = 4,370	10. 7,524 − 2,960 = 4,564	11. 8,015 − 3,677 = 4,338	12. 8,429 − 4,751 = 3,678
13. 7,440 − 5,988 = 1,452	14. 5,038 − 4,832 = 206	15. 7,113 − 4,955 = 2,158	16. 3,665 − 3,444 = 221
17. 7,230 − 4,937 = 2,293	18. 3,825 − 2,125 = 1,700	19. 7,691 − 3,420 = 4,271	20. 4,709 − 3,549 = 1,160
21. 9,110 − 7,625 = 1,485	22. 6,718 − 4,361 = 2,357	23. 7,965 − 4,652 = 3,313	24. 7,619 − 5,475 = 2,144

Page 35

1. 8,545 − 3,388 = 5,157	2. 6,407 − 3,726 = 2,681	3. 8,943 − 5,987 = 2,956	4. 7,487 − 5,320 = 2,167
5. 7,960 − 3,058 = 4,902	6. 6,220 − 4,948 = 1,272	7. 8,148 − 6,584 = 1,564	8. 7,859 − 6,415 = 1,444
9. 8,930 − 8,743 = 187	10. 5,673 − 3,709 = 1,964	11. 8,950 − 4,974 = 3,976	12. 5,922 − 4,096 = 1,826
13. 9,197 − 3,221 = 5,976	14. 6,013 − 4,366 = 1,647	15. 4,167 − 2,304 = 1,863	16. 7,586 − 2,346 = 5,240
17. 8,486 − 7,282 = 1,204	18. 5,582 − 4,723 = 859	19. 6,582 − 2,766 = 3,816	20. 7,949 − 7,246 = 703
21. 8,379 − 4,754 = 3,625	22. 7,546 − 4,943 = 2,603	23. 9,270 − 6,966 = 2,304	24. 6,773 − 5,425 = 1,348

Page 36

1. 7,843 − 6,387 = 1,456	2. 7,135 − 2,178 = 4,957	3. 9,620 − 8,212 = 1,408	4. 9,021 − 3,323 = 5,698
5. 5,020 − 2,161 = 2,859	6. 8,443 − 7,400 = 1,043	7. 6,520 − 6,427 = 93	8. 9,740 − 7,667 = 2,073
9. 6,766 − 4,457 = 2,309	10. 6,563 − 6,316 = 247	11. 3,458 − 2,742 = 716	12. 7,892 − 3,160 = 4,732
13. 8,756 − 3,162 = 5,594	14. 7,357 − 4,849 = 2,508	15. 7,914 − 7,274 = 640	16. 8,143 − 4,850 = 3,293
17. 8,297 − 8,105 = 192	18. 7,751 − 4,708 = 3,043	19. 9,200 − 8,524 = 676	20. 8,426 − 7,281 = 1,145
21. 7,302 − 4,846 = 2,456	22. 8,830 − 5,019 = 3,811	23. 8,319 − 6,586 = 1,733	24. 8,669 − 7,072 = 1,597

Answers
37-40

Set 1 (Subtraction)

1.	2.	3.	4.
8,812 − 4,816 = 3,996	6,731 − 4,003 = 2,728	7,687 − 6,213 = 1,474	6,329 − 4,154 = 2,175
5.	6.	7.	8.
9,064 − 6,892 = 2,172	9,852 − 9,294 = 558	7,114 − 3,996 = 3,118	8,081 − 4,034 = 4,047
9.	10.	11.	12.
7,221 − 3,531 = 3,690	9,586 − 3,755 = 5,831	8,786 − 7,406 = 1,380	6,398 − 5,818 = 580
13.	14.	15.	16.
6,800 − 5,174 = 1,626	6,977 − 3,629 = 3,348	7,233 − 6,879 = 354	8,419 − 2,229 = 6,190
17.	18.	19.	20.
8,648 − 6,023 = 2,625	4,546 − 3,610 = 936	7,070 − 6,420 = 650	7,466 − 6,250 = 1,216
21.	22.	23.	24.
8,251 − 3,434 = 4,817	6,992 − 6,103 = 889	7,880 − 5,275 = 2,605	9,887 − 9,528 = 359

Set 2 (Subtraction)

1.	2.	3.	4.
7,251 − 3,532 = 3,719	6,679 − 2,899 = 3,780	9,106 − 6,918 = 2,188	8,082 − 2,562 = 5,520
5.	6.	7.	8.
9,983 − 5,137 = 4,846	4,928 − 2,461 = 2,467	6,480 − 3,735 = 2,745	6,661 − 4,125 = 2,536
9.	10.	11.	12.
5,683 − 5,242 = 441	9,727 − 2,635 = 7,092	4,713 − 2,675 = 2,038	9,818 − 2,286 = 7,532
13.	14.	15.	16.
5,554 − 2,736 = 2,818	9,044 − 4,196 = 4,848	9,040 − 8,810 = 230	9,819 − 2,398 = 7,421
17.	18.	19.	20.
6,990 − 3,827 = 3,163	9,161 − 7,510 = 1,651	9,495 − 2,249 = 7,246	7,987 − 7,131 = 856
21.	22.	23.	24.
5,223 − 5,216 = 7	7,226 − 3,927 = 3,299	9,552 − 8,759 = 793	3,021 − 2,777 = 244

Set 3 (Multiplication)

1.	2.	3.	4.	5.
2 × 2 = 4	8 × 1 = 8	6 × 1 = 6	9 × 1 = 9	8 × 7 = 56
6.	7.	8.	9.	10.
6 × 5 = 30	7 × 1 = 7	6 × 5 = 30	3 × 7 = 21	6 × 1 = 6
11.	12.	13.	14.	15.
9 × 8 = 72	7 × 4 = 28	7 × 7 = 49	3 × 1 = 3	2 × 8 = 16
16.	17.	18.	19.	20.
7 × 2 = 14	5 × 1 = 5	3 × 6 = 18	2 × 9 = 18	2 × 1 = 2

Set 4 (Multiplication)

1.	2.	3.	4.	5.
1 × 4 = 4	5 × 7 = 35	1 × 8 = 8	4 × 5 = 20	3 × 5 = 15
6.	7.	8.	9.	10.
5 × 1 = 5	8 × 9 = 72	1 × 1 = 1	5 × 5 = 25	2 × 3 = 6
11.	12.	13.	14.	15.
5 × 8 = 40	5 × 3 = 15	1 × 9 = 9	6 × 1 = 6	3 × 8 = 24
16.	17.	18.	19.	20.
6 × 8 = 48	1 × 1 = 1	3 × 4 = 12	4 × 9 = 36	7 × 1 = 7

Answers
41-44

Page 41

1.	2.	3.	4.	5.
8 × 8 = 64	6 × 8 = 48	2 × 1 = 2	9 × 7 = 63	1 × 2 = 2
6.	7.	8.	9.	10.
9 × 4 = 36	6 × 6 = 36	2 × 9 = 18	9 × 4 = 36	1 × 1 = 1
11.	12.	13.	14.	15.
6 × 5 = 30	9 × 1 = 9	8 × 8 = 64	3 × 9 = 27	2 × 5 = 10
16.	17.	18.	19.	20.
9 × 9 = 81	1 × 6 = 6	7 × 7 = 49	5 × 7 = 35	8 × 9 = 72

Page 42

1.	2.	3.	4.	5.
8 × 7 = 56	9 × 1 = 9	8 × 7 = 56	6 × 5 = 30	8 × 5 = 40
6.	7.	8.	9.	10.
9 × 6 = 54	4 × 1 = 4	9 × 9 = 81	8 × 5 = 40	4 × 3 = 12
11.	12.	13.	14.	15.
9 × 1 = 9	1 × 3 = 3	9 × 7 = 63	1 × 7 = 7	3 × 8 = 24
16.	17.	18.	19.	20.
1 × 1 = 1	7 × 8 = 56	2 × 7 = 14	6 × 7 = 42	9 × 1 = 9

Page 43

1.	2.	3.	4.	5.
69 × 97 = 6,693	56 × 57 = 3,192	11 × 30 = 330	75 × 75 = 5,625	22 × 46 = 1,012
6.	7.	8.	9.	10.
45 × 61 = 2,745	53 × 46 = 2,438	23 × 65 = 1,495	50 × 10 = 500	45 × 55 = 2,475
11.	12.	13.	14.	15.
76 × 85 = 6,460	52 × 76 = 3,952	80 × 63 = 5,040	85 × 25 = 2,125	67 × 36 = 2,412
16.	17.	18.	19.	20.
85 × 82 = 6,970	79 × 69 = 5,451	59 × 73 = 4,307	53 × 28 = 1,484	69 × 77 = 5,313
21.	22.	23.	24.	25.
69 × 31 = 2,139	83 × 38 = 3,154	58 × 81 = 4,698	26 × 81 = 2,106	82 × 73 = 5,986
26.	27.	28.	29.	30.
67 × 17 = 1,139	75 × 93 = 6,975	42 × 55 = 2,310	79 × 66 = 5,214	38 × 97 = 3,686

Page 44

1.	2.	3.	4.	5.
60 × 41 = 2,460	71 × 33 = 2,343	31 × 88 = 2,728	44 × 75 = 3,300	49 × 42 = 2,058
6.	7.	8.	9.	10.
11 × 73 = 803	61 × 67 = 4,087	13 × 23 = 299	50 × 17 = 850	11 × 30 = 330
11.	12.	13.	14.	15.
18 × 39 = 702	32 × 21 = 672	16 × 57 = 912	66 × 37 = 2,442	47 × 79 = 3,713
16.	17.	18.	19.	20.
61 × 69 = 4,209	44 × 50 = 2,200	69 × 16 = 1,104	34 × 76 = 2,584	34 × 77 = 2,618
21.	22.	23.	24.	25.
98 × 69 = 6,762	17 × 97 = 1,649	41 × 24 = 984	78 × 57 = 4,446	51 × 23 = 1,173
26.	27.	28.	29.	30.
41 × 60 = 2,460	82 × 53 = 4,346	37 × 40 = 1,480	16 × 27 = 432	27 × 44 = 1,188

Answers
45-48

Set 1 (45)

#	Problem	Answer
1.	65 × 85	5,525
2.	41 × 62	2,542
3.	88 × 12	1,056
4.	68 × 29	1,972
5.	21 × 34	714
6.	60 × 47	2,820
7.	15 × 15	225
8.	39 × 80	3,120
9.	43 × 12	516
10.	65 × 80	5,200
11.	24 × 82	1,968
12.	33 × 50	1,650
13.	44 × 76	3,344
14.	68 × 22	1,496
15.	11 × 62	682
16.	98 × 15	1,470
17.	13 × 78	1,014
18.	89 × 12	1,068
19.	22 × 21	462
20.	57 × 97	5,529
21.	43 × 96	4,128
22.	94 × 42	3,948
23.	16 × 88	1,408
24.	99 × 64	6,336
25.	45 × 27	1,215
26.	81 × 55	4,455
27.	60 × 25	1,500
28.	97 × 81	7,857
29.	74 × 15	1,110
30.	40 × 84	3,360

Set 2 (46)

#	Problem	Answer
1.	71 × 37	2,627
2.	32 × 55	1,760
3.	19 × 41	779
4.	94 × 23	2,162
5.	49 × 93	4,557
6.	69 × 89	6,141
7.	68 × 40	2,720
8.	20 × 39	780
9.	53 × 86	4,558
10.	19 × 46	874
11.	14 × 44	616
12.	43 × 78	3,354
13.	56 × 10	560
14.	52 × 29	1,508
15.	37 × 31	1,147
16.	65 × 19	1,235
17.	68 × 55	3,740
18.	54 × 58	3,132
19.	97 × 67	6,499
20.	97 × 24	2,328
21.	70 × 40	2,800
22.	79 × 85	6,715
23.	97 × 98	9,506
24.	54 × 65	3,510
25.	36 × 51	1,836
26.	99 × 71	7,029
27.	45 × 24	1,080
28.	37 × 51	1,887
29.	54 × 23	1,242
30.	78 × 88	6,864

Set 3 (47)

#	Problem	Answer
1.	99 × 33	3,267
2.	79 × 48	3,792
3.	82 × 74	6,068
4.	71 × 90	6,390
5.	55 × 14	770
6.	19 × 51	969
7.	94 × 14	1,316
8.	36 × 44	1,584
9.	52 × 31	1,612
10.	21 × 24	504
11.	87 × 25	2,175
12.	49 × 44	2,156
13.	62 × 20	1,240
14.	67 × 53	3,551
15.	15 × 38	570
16.	88 × 50	4,400
17.	11 × 68	748
18.	67 × 87	5,829
19.	58 × 59	3,422
20.	33 × 73	2,409
21.	99 × 35	3,465
22.	38 × 53	2,014
23.	37 × 50	1,850
24.	23 × 16	368
25.	27 × 42	1,134
26.	77 × 61	4,697
27.	90 × 49	4,410
28.	19 × 72	1,368
29.	27 × 41	1,107
30.	50 × 52	2,600

Set 4 (48)

#	Problem	Answer
1.	417 × 6	2,502
2.	679 × 10	6,790
3.	344 × 27	9,288
4.	548 × 6	3,288
5.	844 × 11	9,284
6.	278 × 8	2,224
7.	437 × 1	437
8.	586 × 10	5,860
9.	384 × 21	8,064
10.	806 × 12	9,672
11.	271 × 29	7,859
12.	231 × 21	4,851
13.	274 × 20	5,480
14.	387 × 25	9,675
15.	386 × 21	8,106
16.	316 × 12	3,792
17.	649 × 10	6,490
18.	135 × 67	9,045
19.	793 × 1	793
20.	125 × 30	3,750
21.	227 × 23	5,221
22.	122 × 56	6,832
23.	255 × 3	765
24.	374 × 13	4,862
25.	811 × 2	1,622
26.	589 × 11	6,479
27.	457 × 5	2,285
28.	621 × 11	6,831
29.	769 × 6	4,614
30.	146 × 17	2,482

Answers
49-52

49

#	Problem	Answer
1.	140 × 51	7,140
2.	566 × 13	7,358
3.	111 × 77	8,547
4.	288 × 24	6,912
5.	672 × 10	6,720
6.	224 × 26	5,824
7.	125 × 55	6,875
8.	196 × 33	6,468
9.	203 × 4	812
10.	803 × 4	3,212
11.	510 × 15	7,650
12.	323 × 18	5,814
13.	161 × 13	2,093
14.	678 × 11	7,458
15.	118 × 7	826
16.	424 × 7	2,968
17.	817 × 12	9,804
18.	588 × 15	8,820
19.	513 × 15	7,695
20.	998 × 7	6,986
21.	567 × 4	2,268
22.	497 × 14	6,958
23.	929 × 7	6,503
24.	676 × 10	6,760
25.	312 × 30	9,360
26.	132 × 29	3,828
27.	717 × 2	1,434
28.	448 × 22	9,856
29.	780 × 6	4,680
30.	224 × 10	2,240

50

#	Problem	Answer
1.	638 × 10	6,380
2.	111 × 22	2,442
3.	150 × 28	4,200
4.	268 × 23	6,164
5.	285 × 3	855
6.	477 × 7	3,339
7.	519 × 7	3,633
8.	266 × 1	266
9.	150 × 58	8,700
10.	252 × 21	5,292
11.	331 × 6	1,986
12.	426 × 12	5,112
13.	236 × 20	4,720
14.	158 × 3	474
15.	144 × 20	2,880
16.	276 × 2	552
17.	706 × 6	4,236
18.	203 × 15	3,045
19.	331 × 11	3,641
20.	563 × 14	7,882
21.	130 × 6	780
22.	488 × 4	1,952
23.	979 × 4	3,916
24.	582 × 2	1,164
25.	205 × 6	1,230
26.	175 × 17	2,975
27.	156 × 42	6,552
28.	443 × 6	2,658
29.	123 × 69	8,487
30.	256 × 22	5,632

51

#	Problem	Answer
1.	461 × 9	4,149
2.	172 × 47	8,084
3.	320 × 7	2,240
4.	183 × 44	8,052
5.	129 × 72	9,288
6.	437 × 21	9,177
7.	434 × 4	1,736
8.	699 × 6	4,194
9.	145 × 17	2,465
10.	216 × 43	9,288
11.	248 × 19	4,712
12.	193 × 6	1,158
13.	145 × 52	7,540
14.	208 × 29	6,032
15.	772 × 3	2,316
16.	163 × 19	3,097
17.	175 × 56	9,800
18.	217 × 33	7,161
19.	201 × 8	1,608
20.	133 × 26	3,458
21.	230 × 17	3,910
22.	848 × 2	1,696
23.	220 × 25	5,500
24.	552 × 3	1,656
25.	120 × 70	8,400
26.	448 × 1	448
27.	389 × 21	8,169
28.	473 × 13	6,149
29.	186 × 38	7,068
30.	906 × 6	5,436

52

#	Problem	Answer
1.	353 × 15	5,295
2.	203 × 24	4,872
3.	253 × 12	3,036
4.	725 × 5	3,625
5.	140 × 34	4,760
6.	257 × 17	4,369
7.	242 × 27	6,534
8.	236 × 12	2,832
9.	465 × 10	4,650
10.	386 × 8	3,088
11.	733 × 9	6,597
12.	258 × 1	258
13.	834 × 7	5,838
14.	193 × 43	8,299
15.	400 × 7	2,800
16.	568 × 2	1,136
17.	176 × 14	2,464
18.	597 × 5	2,985
19.	683 × 13	8,879
20.	405 × 9	3,645
21.	146 × 46	6,716
22.	237 × 22	5,214
23.	145 × 13	1,885
24.	589 × 10	5,890
25.	334 × 7	2,338
26.	816 × 5	4,080
27.	158 × 39	6,162
28.	809 × 1	809
29.	133 × 10	1,330
30.	679 × 13	8,827

Answers
53-56

Set 1

1.	2.	3.	4.
5,621 × 92 = 517,132	8,211 × 83 = 681,513	2,769 × 98 = 271,362	2,567 × 45 = 115,515
5.	6.	7.	8.
4,782 × 75 = 358,650	8,796 × 79 = 694,884	5,981 × 67 = 400,727	4,238 × 60 = 254,280
9.	10.	11.	12.
5,592 × 69 = 385,848	4,291 × 15 = 64,365	7,822 × 61 = 477,142	9,684 × 71 = 687,564
13.	14.	15.	16.
4,059 × 88 = 357,192	9,876 × 59 = 582,684	2,100 × 42 = 88,200	5,515 × 35 = 193,025
17.	18.	19.	20.
9,277 × 91 = 844,207	2,277 × 49 = 111,573	4,293 × 16 = 68,688	3,428 × 90 = 308,520
21.	22.	23.	24.
3,859 × 37 = 142,783	6,769 × 68 = 460,292	4,161 × 78 = 324,558	9,332 × 92 = 858,544

Set 2

1.	2.	3.	4.
9,817 × 20 = 196,340	9,487 × 42 = 398,454	8,943 × 65 = 581,295	1,758 × 59 = 103,722
5.	6.	7.	8.
7,077 × 86 = 608,622	5,130 × 50 = 256,500	7,641 × 39 = 297,999	4,916 × 48 = 235,968
9.	10.	11.	12.
3,973 × 26 = 103,298	7,761 × 88 = 682,968	6,852 × 38 = 260,376	5,100 × 49 = 249,900
13.	14.	15.	16.
7,833 × 25 = 195,825	7,193 × 63 = 453,159	2,931 × 91 = 266,721	5,035 × 55 = 276,925
17.	18.	19.	20.
4,827 × 49 = 236,523	5,726 × 19 = 108,794	9,405 × 35 = 329,175	7,781 × 42 = 326,802
21.	22.	23.	24.
9,745 × 41 = 399,545	4,108 × 62 = 254,696	5,268 × 82 = 431,976	7,627 × 78 = 594,906

Set 3

1.	2.	3.	4.
2,722 × 13 = 35,386	8,845 × 11 = 97,295	6,764 × 19 = 128,516	4,313 × 88 = 379,544
5.	6.	7.	8.
9,689 × 14 = 135,646	4,835 × 41 = 198,235	3,558 × 29 = 103,182	5,430 × 99 = 537,570
9.	10.	11.	12.
5,545 × 89 = 493,505	5,841 × 32 = 186,912	2,737 × 76 = 208,012	9,196 × 39 = 358,644
13.	14.	15.	16.
3,373 × 73 = 246,229	5,164 × 50 = 258,200	6,949 × 30 = 208,470	3,777 × 34 = 128,418
17.	18.	19.	20.
1,717 × 67 = 115,039	2,362 × 75 = 177,150	3,067 × 88 = 269,896	3,479 × 19 = 66,101
21.	22.	23.	24.
8,804 × 79 = 695,516	6,923 × 53 = 366,919	7,629 × 90 = 686,610	8,346 × 20 = 166,920

Set 4

1.	2.	3.	4.
4,407 × 97 = 427,479	6,827 × 53 = 361,831	4,052 × 50 = 202,600	5,752 × 83 = 477,416
5.	6.	7.	8.
2,852 × 76 = 216,752	4,731 × 33 = 156,123	4,804 × 78 = 374,712	4,828 × 52 = 251,056
9.	10.	11.	12.
4,922 × 92 = 452,824	7,007 × 11 = 77,077	5,229 × 52 = 271,908	8,156 × 77 = 628,012
13.	14.	15.	16.
8,777 × 47 = 412,519	2,945 × 79 = 232,655	2,330 × 19 = 44,270	9,889 × 62 = 613,118
17.	18.	19.	20.
3,402 × 18 = 61,236	3,592 × 73 = 262,216	6,321 × 84 = 530,964	2,835 × 12 = 34,020
21.	22.	23.	24.
7,388 × 37 = 273,356	3,436 × 10 = 34,360	6,203 × 92 = 570,676	3,187 × 88 = 280,456

Answers
57-60

Box 1

1.	2.	3.	4.
2,067 × 99 = 204,633	4,067 × 77 = 313,159	7,344 × 78 = 572,832	2,945 × 43 = 126,635

5.	6.	7.	8.
6,148 × 28 = 172,144	3,352 × 93 = 311,736	2,938 × 94 = 276,172	4,957 × 24 = 118,968

9.	10.	11.	12.
3,443 × 30 = 103,290	2,247 × 26 = 58,422	9,043 × 41 = 370,763	4,846 × 61 = 295,606

13.	14.	15.	16.
6,723 × 62 = 416,826	1,876 × 40 = 75,040	8,795 × 42 = 369,390	2,539 × 99 = 251,361

17.	18.	19.	20.
2,696 × 33 = 88,968	4,538 × 83 = 376,654	4,767 × 73 = 347,991	2,914 × 24 = 69,936

21.	22.	23.	24.
5,146 × 84 = 432,264	2,166 × 49 = 106,134	4,976 × 32 = 159,232	5,318 × 72 = 382,896

Box 2

1.	2.	3.	4.	5.
6 ÷ 1 = 6	9 ÷ 9 = 1	10 ÷ 2 = 5	5 ÷ 5 = 1	7 ÷ 7 = 1

6.	7.	8.	9.	10.
14 ÷ 2 = 7	18 ÷ 6 = 3	6 ÷ 3 = 2	8 ÷ 2 = 4	14 ÷ 2 = 7

11.	12.	13.	14.	15.
8 ÷ 8 = 1	12 ÷ 2 = 6	15 ÷ 5 = 3	9 ÷ 9 = 1	16 ÷ 4 = 4

16.	17.	18.	19.	20.
7 ÷ 7 = 1	12 ÷ 2 = 6	20 ÷ 4 = 5	7 ÷ 7 = 1	12 ÷ 3 = 4

Box 3

1.	2.	3.	4.	5.
15 ÷ 5 = 3	8 ÷ 2 = 4	16 ÷ 4 = 4	20 ÷ 4 = 5	12 ÷ 2 = 6

6.	7.	8.	9.	10.
20 ÷ 1 = 20	18 ÷ 2 = 9	6 ÷ 1 = 6	14 ÷ 2 = 7	12 ÷ 6 = 2

11.	12.	13.	14.	15.
8 ÷ 4 = 2	12 ÷ 6 = 2	1 ÷ 1 = 1	3 ÷ 3 = 1	5 ÷ 1 = 5

16.	17.	18.	19.	20.
17 ÷ 1 = 17	16 ÷ 8 = 2	7 ÷ 7 = 1	13 ÷ 1 = 13	12 ÷ 3 = 4

Box 4

1.	2.	3.	4.	5.
8 ÷ 8 = 1	9 ÷ 9 = 1	18 ÷ 9 = 2	7 ÷ 7 = 1	16 ÷ 8 = 2

6.	7.	8.	9.	10.
14 ÷ 7 = 2	12 ÷ 6 = 2	7 ÷ 7 = 1	11 ÷ 1 = 11	18 ÷ 2 = 9

11.	12.	13.	14.	15.
6 ÷ 1 = 6	10 ÷ 5 = 2	10 ÷ 5 = 2	15 ÷ 5 = 3	9 ÷ 3 = 3

16.	17.	18.	19.	20.
12 ÷ 3 = 4	15 ÷ 5 = 3	12 ÷ 4 = 3	14 ÷ 7 = 2	6 ÷ 3 = 2

Answers
61-64

Worksheet 61

1. 15 ÷ 3 = 5
2. 8 ÷ 8 = 1
3. 7 ÷ 7 = 1
4. 12 ÷ 4 = 3
5. 10 ÷ 5 = 2
6. 4 ÷ 2 = 2
7. 12 ÷ 3 = 4
8. 15 ÷ 1 = 15
9. 11 ÷ 1 = 11
10. 7 ÷ 7 = 1
11. 8 ÷ 8 = 1
12. 15 ÷ 5 = 3
13. 18 ÷ 1 = 18
14. 10 ÷ 5 = 2
15. 6 ÷ 6 = 1
16. 16 ÷ 8 = 2
17. 6 ÷ 6 = 1
18. 10 ÷ 2 = 5
19. 5 ÷ 1 = 5
20. 15 ÷ 3 = 5

Worksheet 62

1. 34 ÷ 2 = 17
2. 74 ÷ 1 = 74
3. 18 ÷ 9 = 2
4. 87 ÷ 1 = 87
5. 84 ÷ 6 = 14
6. 77 ÷ 7 = 11
7. 84 ÷ 6 = 14
8. 52 ÷ 2 = 26
9. 81 ÷ 9 = 9
10. 88 ÷ 8 = 11
11. 36 ÷ 6 = 6
12. 18 ÷ 6 = 3
13. 48 ÷ 6 = 8
14. 63 ÷ 7 = 9
15. 63 ÷ 9 = 7
16. 49 ÷ 7 = 7
17. 28 ÷ 7 = 4
18. 24 ÷ 6 = 4
19. 36 ÷ 6 = 6
20. 40 ÷ 8 = 5
21. 60 ÷ 3 = 20
22. 28 ÷ 2 = 14
23. 86 ÷ 2 = 43
24. 18 ÷ 9 = 2
25. 36 ÷ 9 = 4
26. 54 ÷ 3 = 18
27. 45 ÷ 9 = 5
28. 95 ÷ 5 = 19
29. 40 ÷ 5 = 8
30. 40 ÷ 8 = 5

Worksheet 63

1. 56 ÷ 8 = 7
2. 84 ÷ 4 = 21
3. 57 ÷ 1 = 57
4. 32 ÷ 8 = 4
5. 60 ÷ 4 = 15
6. 81 ÷ 1 = 81
7. 57 ÷ 3 = 19
8. 16 ÷ 8 = 2
9. 15 ÷ 3 = 5
10. 24 ÷ 6 = 4
11. 48 ÷ 8 = 6
12. 24 ÷ 8 = 3
13. 14 ÷ 7 = 2
14. 35 ÷ 7 = 5
15. 82 ÷ 1 = 82
16. 63 ÷ 7 = 9
17. 30 ÷ 5 = 6
18. 31 ÷ 1 = 31
19. 42 ÷ 7 = 6
20. 32 ÷ 8 = 4
21. 52 ÷ 4 = 13
22. 96 ÷ 8 = 12
23. 63 ÷ 3 = 21
24. 90 ÷ 6 = 15
25. 48 ÷ 6 = 8
26. 36 ÷ 2 = 18
27. 57 ÷ 3 = 19
28. 14 ÷ 2 = 7
29. 56 ÷ 8 = 7
30. 97 ÷ 1 = 97

Worksheet 64

1. 81 ÷ 3 = 27
2. 24 ÷ 8 = 3
3. 44 ÷ 1 = 44
4. 15 ÷ 3 = 5
5. 78 ÷ 6 = 13
6. 45 ÷ 9 = 5
7. 24 ÷ 6 = 4
8. 16 ÷ 4 = 4
9. 42 ÷ 7 = 6
10. 36 ÷ 1 = 36
11. 33 ÷ 3 = 11
12. 38 ÷ 2 = 19
13. 27 ÷ 9 = 3
14. 45 ÷ 9 = 5
15. 36 ÷ 9 = 4
16. 40 ÷ 5 = 8
17. 80 ÷ 8 = 10
18. 64 ÷ 8 = 8
19. 35 ÷ 7 = 5
20. 80 ÷ 8 = 10
21. 30 ÷ 5 = 6
22. 11 ÷ 1 = 11
23. 62 ÷ 1 = 62
24. 30 ÷ 6 = 5
25. 88 ÷ 8 = 11
26. 16 ÷ 8 = 2
27. 72 ÷ 6 = 12
28. 36 ÷ 4 = 9
29. 88 ÷ 8 = 11
30. 81 ÷ 9 = 9

Answers
65-68

Set 1 (65)

#	Problem	Answer
1.	40 ÷ 8	5
2.	42 ÷ 6	7
3.	55 ÷ 5	11
4.	35 ÷ 5	7
5.	42 ÷ 6	7
6.	92 ÷ 4	23
7.	16 ÷ 1	16
8.	83 ÷ 1	83
9.	84 ÷ 6	14
10.	16 ÷ 1	16
11.	78 ÷ 6	13
12.	42 ÷ 1	42
13.	45 ÷ 9	5
14.	68 ÷ 2	34
15.	12 ÷ 6	2
16.	84 ÷ 3	28
17.	14 ÷ 2	7
18.	90 ÷ 9	10
19.	68 ÷ 4	17
20.	72 ÷ 8	9
21.	48 ÷ 8	6
22.	28 ÷ 2	14
23.	60 ÷ 5	12
24.	86 ÷ 2	43
25.	98 ÷ 7	14
26.	44 ÷ 4	11
27.	48 ÷ 4	12
28.	63 ÷ 7	9
29.	56 ÷ 4	14
30.	44 ÷ 1	44

Set 2 (66)

#	Problem	Answer
1.	28 ÷ 7	4
2.	90 ÷ 5	18
3.	62 ÷ 1	62
4.	84 ÷ 4	21
5.	12 ÷ 1	12
6.	42 ÷ 7	6
7.	28 ÷ 4	7
8.	36 ÷ 3	12
9.	65 ÷ 5	13
10.	90 ÷ 2	45
11.	80 ÷ 5	16
12.	65 ÷ 1	65
13.	81 ÷ 9	9
14.	80 ÷ 2	40
15.	30 ÷ 3	10
16.	27 ÷ 9	3
17.	87 ÷ 3	29
18.	49 ÷ 7	7
19.	72 ÷ 6	12
20.	80 ÷ 1	80
21.	28 ÷ 7	4
22.	36 ÷ 4	9
23.	48 ÷ 4	12
24.	21 ÷ 3	7
25.	76 ÷ 1	76
26.	22 ÷ 1	22
27.	64 ÷ 8	8
28.	54 ÷ 2	27
29.	54 ÷ 2	27
30.	21 ÷ 3	7

Set 3 (67)

#	Problem	Answer
1.	720 ÷ 80	9
2.	690 ÷ 46	15
3.	186 ÷ 62	3
4.	814 ÷ 37	22
5.	426 ÷ 71	6
6.	840 ÷ 70	12
7.	840 ÷ 60	14
8.	140 ÷ 70	2
9.	987 ÷ 47	21
10.	624 ÷ 24	26
11.	675 ÷ 25	27
12.	819 ÷ 21	39
13.	396 ÷ 18	22
14.	882 ÷ 63	14
15.	840 ÷ 5	168
16.	172 ÷ 86	2
17.	459 ÷ 27	17
18.	730 ÷ 73	10
19.	540 ÷ 54	10
20.	686 ÷ 98	7
21.	900 ÷ 15	60
22.	969 ÷ 19	51
23.	456 ÷ 57	8
24.	760 ÷ 38	20
25.	630 ÷ 70	9
26.	374 ÷ 17	22
27.	348 ÷ 58	6
28.	440 ÷ 10	44
29.	368 ÷ 92	4
30.	488 ÷ 61	8

Set 4 (68)

#	Problem	Answer
1.	985 ÷ 5	197
2.	588 ÷ 98	6
3.	532 ÷ 19	28
4.	648 ÷ 81	8
5.	120 ÷ 60	2
6.	666 ÷ 74	9
7.	425 ÷ 85	5
8.	836 ÷ 19	44
9.	285 ÷ 95	3
10.	605 ÷ 55	11
11.	140 ÷ 5	28
12.	550 ÷ 50	11
13.	784 ÷ 98	8
14.	924 ÷ 77	12
15.	550 ÷ 11	50
16.	440 ÷ 40	11
17.	728 ÷ 56	13
18.	868 ÷ 4	217
19.	216 ÷ 8	27
20.	388 ÷ 97	4
21.	594 ÷ 66	9
22.	171 ÷ 57	3
23.	660 ÷ 66	10
24.	936 ÷ 72	13
25.	729 ÷ 81	9
26.	291 ÷ 97	3
27.	776 ÷ 8	97
28.	396 ÷ 36	11
29.	333 ÷ 9	37
30.	351 ÷ 13	27

Box 1 (left top):

1. 611 ÷ 47 = 13	2. 800 ÷ 80 = 10	3. 469 ÷ 67 = 7	4. 273 ÷ 39 = 7	5. 552 ÷ 92 = 6
6. 742 ÷ 53 = 14	7. 315 ÷ 45 = 7	8. 792 ÷ 99 = 8	9. 376 ÷ 94 = 4	10. 594 ÷ 27 = 22
11. 570 ÷ 57 = 10	12. 616 ÷ 77 = 8	13. 448 ÷ 14 = 32	14. 320 ÷ 64 = 5	15. 249 ÷ 83 = 3
16. 400 ÷ 1 = 400	17. 352 ÷ 16 = 22	18. 810 ÷ 54 = 15	19. 360 ÷ 60 = 6	20. 924 ÷ 42 = 22
21. 264 ÷ 88 = 3	22. 119 ÷ 17 = 7	23. 600 ÷ 15 = 40	24. 702 ÷ 27 = 26	25. 267 ÷ 3 = 89
26. 147 ÷ 49 = 3	27. 798 ÷ 57 = 14	28. 304 ÷ 76 = 4	29. 488 ÷ 4 = 122	30. 984 ÷ 41 = 24

Box 2 (right top):

1. 261 ÷ 87 = 3	2. 680 ÷ 85 = 8	3. 210 ÷ 21 = 10	4. 544 ÷ 32 = 17	5. 750 ÷ 75 = 10
6. 429 ÷ 13 = 33	7. 680 ÷ 68 = 10	8. 732 ÷ 12 = 61	9. 204 ÷ 68 = 3	10. 672 ÷ 84 = 8
11. 294 ÷ 98 = 3	12. 160 ÷ 20 = 8	13. 708 ÷ 59 = 12	14. 915 ÷ 61 = 15	15. 476 ÷ 34 = 14
16. 776 ÷ 97 = 8	17. 476 ÷ 68 = 7	18. 477 ÷ 53 = 9	19. 261 ÷ 87 = 3	20. 294 ÷ 6 = 49
21. 255 ÷ 15 = 17	22. 406 ÷ 58 = 7	23. 225 ÷ 75 = 3	24. 452 ÷ 1 = 452	25. 540 ÷ 90 = 6
26. 790 ÷ 79 = 10	27. 624 ÷ 26 = 24	28. 620 ÷ 31 = 20	29. 319 ÷ 29 = 11	30. 352 ÷ 88 = 4

Box 3 (left bottom):

1. 658 ÷ 7 = 94	2. 990 ÷ 45 = 22	3. 768 ÷ 96 = 8	4. 462 ÷ 42 = 11	5. 120 ÷ 15 = 8
6. 986 ÷ 58 = 17	7. 520 ÷ 20 = 26	8. 748 ÷ 22 = 34	9. 486 ÷ 54 = 9	10. 696 ÷ 87 = 8
11. 783 ÷ 87 = 9	12. 560 ÷ 80 = 7	13. 324 ÷ 9 = 36	14. 882 ÷ 42 = 21	15. 350 ÷ 50 = 7
16. 697 ÷ 41 = 17	17. 976 ÷ 16 = 61	18. 840 ÷ 28 = 30	19. 237 ÷ 79 = 3	20. 768 ÷ 48 = 16
21. 144 ÷ 24 = 6	22. 920 ÷ 46 = 20	23. 806 ÷ 62 = 13	24. 880 ÷ 88 = 10	25. 282 ÷ 6 = 47
26. 828 ÷ 36 = 23	27. 425 ÷ 85 = 5	28. 518 ÷ 74 = 7	29. 936 ÷ 78 = 12	30. 810 ÷ 27 = 30

Box 4 (right bottom):

1. 4,108 ÷ 26 = 158	2. 6,944 ÷ 16 = 434	3. 6,384 ÷ 16 = 399	4. 5,376 ÷ 32 = 168
5. 5,766 ÷ 93 = 62	6. 7,268 ÷ 23 = 316	7. 6,348 ÷ 46 = 138	8. 9,504 ÷ 54 = 176
9. 9,541 ÷ 29 = 329	10. 3,150 ÷ 45 = 70	11. 6,956 ÷ 47 = 148	12. 9,135 ÷ 21 = 435
13. 8,624 ÷ 11 = 784	14. 7,124 ÷ 52 = 137	15. 3,050 ÷ 25 = 122	16. 6,708 ÷ 26 = 258
17. 1,725 ÷ 23 = 75	18. 2,714 ÷ 46 = 59	19. 8,730 ÷ 15 = 582	20. 3,519 ÷ 69 = 51
21. 3,575 ÷ 65 = 55	22. 7,260 ÷ 44 = 165	23. 5,075 ÷ 25 = 203	24. 1,856 ÷ 64 = 29

Answers
73-76

Page 73

#	Problem	Answer
1.	5,402 ÷ 37	146
2.	5,448 ÷ 24	227
3.	7,423 ÷ 13	571
4.	9,500 ÷ 95	100
5.	8,610 ÷ 70	123
6.	5,928 ÷ 78	76
7.	8,432 ÷ 17	496
8.	7,242 ÷ 71	102
9.	4,209 ÷ 61	69
10.	9,516 ÷ 78	122
11.	4,968 ÷ 69	72
12.	5,032 ÷ 74	68
13.	4,420 ÷ 65	68
14.	4,588 ÷ 31	148
15.	2,850 ÷ 38	75
16.	8,395 ÷ 73	115
17.	9,823 ÷ 47	209
18.	4,316 ÷ 83	52
19.	3,045 ÷ 87	35
20.	7,868 ÷ 14	562
21.	7,938 ÷ 54	147
22.	6,279 ÷ 69	91
23.	8,170 ÷ 95	86
24.	9,193 ÷ 29	317

Page 74

#	Problem	Answer
1.	2,640 ÷ 40	66
2.	7,776 ÷ 96	81
3.	2,480 ÷ 62	40
4.	6,720 ÷ 80	84
5.	6,405 ÷ 61	105
6.	8,395 ÷ 73	115
7.	9,212 ÷ 98	94
8.	7,640 ÷ 10	764
9.	2,698 ÷ 71	38
10.	5,632 ÷ 64	88
11.	7,028 ÷ 14	502
12.	5,810 ÷ 83	70
13.	5,986 ÷ 82	73
14.	5,735 ÷ 31	185
15.	6,900 ÷ 23	300
16.	4,095 ÷ 65	63
17.	2,790 ÷ 45	62
18.	4,074 ÷ 14	291
19.	8,050 ÷ 70	115
20.	5,684 ÷ 98	58
21.	2,240 ÷ 20	112
22.	8,342 ÷ 97	86
23.	4,089 ÷ 87	47
24.	3,276 ÷ 18	182

Page 75

#	Problem	Answer
1.	2,255 ÷ 55	41
2.	1,872 ÷ 39	48
3.	7,200 ÷ 48	150
4.	8,960 ÷ 70	128
5.	2,835 ÷ 63	45
6.	8,178 ÷ 58	141
7.	4,374 ÷ 81	54
8.	9,555 ÷ 39	245
9.	6,804 ÷ 28	243
10.	7,275 ÷ 97	75
11.	6,444 ÷ 12	537
12.	6,665 ÷ 31	215
13.	6,580 ÷ 28	235
14.	4,180 ÷ 55	76
15.	2,175 ÷ 29	75
16.	9,636 ÷ 66	146
17.	9,540 ÷ 36	265
18.	5,115 ÷ 55	93
19.	8,246 ÷ 38	217
20.	2,783 ÷ 23	121
21.	8,316 ÷ 28	297
22.	8,372 ÷ 91	92
23.	7,860 ÷ 10	786
24.	8,280 ÷ 69	120

Page 76

#	Problem	Answer
1.	2,385 ÷ 53	45
2.	7,720 ÷ 40	193
3.	3,900 ÷ 75	52
4.	8,547 ÷ 77	111
5.	1,936 ÷ 88	22
6.	8,908 ÷ 68	131
7.	4,664 ÷ 88	53
8.	6,776 ÷ 28	242
9.	7,150 ÷ 65	110
10.	9,460 ÷ 86	110
11.	5,640 ÷ 94	60
12.	5,922 ÷ 94	63
13.	1,817 ÷ 79	23
14.	7,990 ÷ 34	235
15.	8,740 ÷ 76	115
16.	7,068 ÷ 38	186
17.	8,640 ÷ 36	240
18.	5,985 ÷ 21	285
19.	9,486 ÷ 93	102
20.	3,441 ÷ 37	93
21.	2,550 ÷ 17	150
22.	5,871 ÷ 57	103
23.	9,792 ÷ 68	144
24.	5,304 ÷ 52	102

Answers
77

1. 7,387 ÷ 83 = 89	**2.** 9,440 ÷ 20 = 472	**3.** 5,833 ÷ 19 = 307	**4.** 5,727 ÷ 69 = 83
5. 6,594 ÷ 21 = 314	**6.** 9,600 ÷ 80 = 120	**7.** 3,120 ÷ 60 = 52	**8.** 6,105 ÷ 55 = 111
9. 9,225 ÷ 25 = 369	**10.** 1,344 ÷ 28 = 48	**11.** 7,956 ÷ 68 = 117	**12.** 2,496 ÷ 48 = 52
13. 5,018 ÷ 13 = 386	**14.** 6,468 ÷ 66 = 98	**15.** 8,175 ÷ 25 = 327	**16.** 8,721 ÷ 27 = 323
17. 9,120 ÷ 96 = 95	**18.** 7,524 ÷ 76 = 99	**19.** 7,968 ÷ 96 = 83	**20.** 1,368 ÷ 76 = 18
21. 9,266 ÷ 82 = 113	**22.** 3,050 ÷ 61 = 50	**23.** 2,226 ÷ 53 = 42	**24.** 9,100 ÷ 50 = 182

www.ingramcontent.com/pod-product-compliance
Lightning Source LLC
Chambersburg PA
CBHW060122120726
48003CB00009B/2745